M000309436

THE FRONT OFFICE

A Guide to Hedge Funds for Retail,

Day Traders, and Aspiring Quants

Tom Costello

Introduction

In 2019, a year of more or less average performance for the financial markets, the hedge fund industry collectively extracted 224 Billion dollars in profit and kept 37.4 Billon of it for themselves. They've done a similar thing every year, for well over 20 years. To put a sense of scale to that, right now Wikipedia lists the Annual GDP of Greece and New Zealand at 209 Billion, and 206 Billion, respectively. Slightly less than hedge fund industry returns.

The average annualized performance of a hedge fund in 2019 was about 11%. But what's often missed in the press when they talk about averages, is that there is a huge and persistent gap between the best performing hedge funds and the worst performing, which makes the average performance a meaningless statistic. More helpful is the knowledge that the return profile of the hedge fund industry is a Pareto distribution, and something close to 80% of that 224 Billion in yearly profits came from the largest 20% of hedge funds, who seem to have a distinct advantage over everyone else.

The worst hedge fund performers, who are also almost always the smallest, lost money overall. They do so every year. But believing that their poor performance is caused by their smallness gets the cause and effect wrong. It's considerably easier to manage a small amount of money than a large one. The most common reason those small hedge funds are small and stay small, is because they don't understand the markets in the same way that the larger funds all do, so they never get to the same level of profitability. If they did, the market would be only too happy to see them grow.

On almost any topic, there is a great deal of diversity of opinion in the hedge fund world. But there are some ideas that everyone in that top 20% have in common, and those ideas are almost never shared by the bottom 80%. The leaders share a perspective on how to look at the markets in order to find an opportunity. It's a view that lays out which kinds of ideas to invest time and energy in exploiting, and which kinds of ideas to reject or ignore.

Those of us who got our experience at the top tier were all taught it, but we almost never talk about it. I've never seen it successfully explained anywhere in print, and with 30 years in the business talking almost exclusively to money managers and those who aspire to the role, I've never met anyone who taught it to themselves. But it's often whether someone can both understand this perspective and convey an understanding of it to others, that's the determining factor in whether they're viewed as a hedge fund insider or an outsider.

To be a bit more precise, this view is a perspective on what markets are, how they work, and what the most reliable way to think about them is if you want to exploit them for gain. It can be described as the intellectual and philosophical underpinnings which support the thinking of the top performers of the hedge fund industry. As far as I've been able to tell, the only way that people can acquire a working knowledge of these concepts, is by spending time in the industry itself.

Thanks in part to declining standards in education, this perspective certainly isn't immediately intuitive to you if you haven't. And because it isn't, those who are self-trained in the financial markets never seem to find it on their own. Instead, they waste a spectacular amount of time chasing what to leaders in the space, look like obvious dead ends.

I don't want you to get the wrong idea. I'm not talking about some closely guarded secret that's only revealed to you during some pseudo-religious rite in an investment bank basement, after you pledge your eternal soul to the gods of Davos. It's nothing like that. And it isn't technical information either. All the mathematical information on how to price an option or bootstrap a yield curve is all available on the internet for free. If you can afford to invest in a Bloomberg terminal, they'll do all the technical math for you.

What I'm talking about is how all that information is all tied together and what that should mean to you if you want to turn as reliable and as large a profit as the leaders in the space. A winning hedge fund thinks about markets in ways that makes them more likely to win. And that means that at some level their thought processes are similar, regardless of the specific strategies they pursue.

For me, the difference in perspective is deeply reminiscent of the parable of the blind monks seeing an elephant for the first time. One touches its leg and declares it to be like a tree, another touches its trunk and declares it to be like a snake, a third touches it's side and claims that it's like a boulder. They're all telling people the truth, and none are completely wrong given the portion they're exposed to. But none are seeing the whole creature. To those of us who came up on the institutional side of the markets, it looks very much like most people get their trading instruction only from blind monks.

By far the most common error of the self-taught is the belief that the smart people win and the dumb people lose. The gap between the best and the worst performers is definitely not a matter of intelligence. There are lots of brilliant people outside the institutional finance industry, and a great many people within it who are of no more than average intelligence. Smarter is not the secret. But the people in the largest institutions do have different knowledge than the self-taught. They're seeing connections which the blind monks offering advice to everyone else never seem to.

Some of those blind monks will tell you that the market is about understanding animal spirits. Others will tell you the benefits of sector rotation, or value investing, or the technical shape of some chart. Some will insist it's all about balance sheet assessment or economic analysis. All of those things are perfectly valid parts of the market, but none of them describes the whole thing. I'm going to ty to explain how, to the people who have achieved the highest levels of success in the hedge fund world, the elephant that is the market, looks exactly like an elephant.

I'm firmly convinced that there is no domain in the modern world where the Dunning-Kruger effect is more common than the stock market. If you're one of those people who has come by some trading expertise, then you've probably seen it too. Even though a great many people, maybe even a majority, believe they completely understand how markets work, if they did, there would be no hedge fund industry at all, let alone one that consistently takes 224 Billion a year from other people, year, after year, after year. I'm going to explain to you how they do that. I'm going to share the perspective that I learned working with and for them, in the hope that you can add your best effort to the process, and maybe do as well as they do.

This is not an entry level book. It's a book for the self-taught so it contains some very basic concepts as support for more complex ideas, but if you don't already understand the basic goals of trading for a living, you might not get much out of it. It's really a book for someone who thinks, or at least hopes, they might be ready to take a shot at getting into the hedge fund world. Those are the people I've had my direct experience with, and this book speaks to the issues that I know people in that position most often miss.

This book contains almost no math, but it's not for the innumerate. I left all but the most basic math out because there are a million other places you can find that instruction for free from someone who can probably explain it better than I can. After 30 years as a quant, I'm hardly innumerate either, but I'm in no danger of winning a Fields Medal. The math does matter though, so hopefully you'll be inspired to look into it on your own.

I'm also not giving you a 'sure fire trading model'. Anyone who promises you something like that is lying to you. In the institutional capital markets, no one ever gives you anything of real value for free.

I'm going to give you a window into some concepts that will help you see the difference between a genuine opportunity and a false one. And I'll do my best to explain the thought processes that lead to that kind of differentiation. There are only a few paths that lead to success in the hedge fund world and an uncountable number of paths that don't. If you can read between the lines and see the sometimes-circuitous connections I lay out, then hopefully that's enough to put you on the right path.

As I'll say repeatedly, understanding markets is really about understanding people. You can't really predict what an individual person will do with any accuracy. But the behavior of a group of people can be predicted to some greater or lesser degree. I've been doing this my entire adult life so as an example, let me tell you what I think is probably true about the group of people who make up the potential readers of this book.

Everyone who reads this book will have a few things in common. You will all be of above average intelligence. Maybe considerably above average. People who are below average don't typically have this kind of ambition. You will be engaged in, or have already acquired a STEM related degree. I'd expect slightly greater interest from Tech majors than from Business majors, but the younger the reader the more the odds will even. Maybe you're working in another area of finance. Maybe retail brokerage, asset management, or some support role someplace, and you want to get to where the big money is made. But by far, the most important thing you all have in common is what life managing money in a hedge fund represents to you.

I think to people in the typical reader's position, life in a hedge fund represents a level of control over your own life and your own future. It's a chance for you to make a very good living based on what you alone bring to the table, and where you won't be dependent on anyone else or anyone else's goodwill. Where there's no huge organization standing between you and goals – just you, your wits, and the objective markets. I think you're looking for a way that you can be truly independent and be in full control of your own life. in the process, you also might get very, very rich.

Unlike many of the other assumptions that you're probably

making about hedge funds, all of those are absolutely true. Life in a hedge fund definitely offers those things and though it's both a blessing and a curse in ways I'll explain, if you manage to break into it you will very much be living and dying by your decision making alone. You may have help, but no one will do it for you.

But between here and there, there are more than a few other misconceptions about what the hedge fund world is like, that we'll need to correct. The sooner you understand and embrace them, the easier I think it will be for you.

Common Misconceptions

I think I can say without fear of reasonable contradiction, that the hedge fund industry is the most hated industry in the world. It's despised and envied by the press, thoughtlessly (often stupidly) caricatured in film and TV, and demonized by politicians on both the left and right, both large and small. It's no industry to get into if you're worried about being popular.

If you chose to enter it anyway, some people will wish you dead for no reason other than your career choice. You'll get called a thief and a liar by people who have never met you. Entire political movements will exist for no purpose other than seeing you punished. For what specifically? They have no idea... but something. And though they'll probably never think it through, they'll still take the time to send you online death threats or to demand prison time for you on twitter, even when you're strictly obeying the letter of every law and regulation.

With a few notable exceptions, hedge fund staffers and Bankers in general, are portrayed either as idiotic overgrown frat boys, high fiving each other as they steal money from widows and orphans, or as narcissistic deviants who get through their day consuming huge piles of cocaine, and their nights throwing parties filled with expensive hookers and dwarf tossing. This is nonsense.

It's nothing more than a dark, silly fantasy, created by screenwriters who have never been within 5 miles of a real hedge fund, and who don't know the first thing about it.

Much of what you saw in "The Wolf of Wall Street" may have really happened. But while that sort of thing was going on at the seediest end of Wall Street, the most talented part of the hedge fund industry was hard at work at the other end. Institutional trading has as little in common with a bunch of nearly illiterate stock brokers scamming their retail clients, as driving a bus on the NJ Turnpike does with trying to win the Monaco Grand Prix. For most of the hedge fund industry this is deadly serious, deeply challenging work, from which a large portion of the general public derive, at least an indirect benefit.

In the real world, you may read an occasional news story about some young hedge fund staffer whose party in a rented Hamptons house got out of control, or of someone here or there accused of insider trading. That happens infrequently. But if you ask me, those stories are notable for their rarity. Any group of people as large as the hedge fund industry is bound to have a few bad apples.

But it's very uncommon because that's not how the vast majority of the industry works. There are plenty of people working in hedge funds who would do that sort of thing every weekend if they could. It's no more a monastery than the Entertainment industry, or Silicon Valley. But the reason it doesn't happen very often, is because for the most part it can't. And that's because of what the hedge fund industry really is.

What the hedge fund industry runs on more than anything else, is credibility. To be even moderately successful, you need to present a credible picture to the people in control of the largest pools of assets in the world. You need to persuade the people who manage those assets that you will protect their money from loss, while also presenting a careful, well-reasoned argument for why allowing you to manage it for them will result in greater profits.

You need to be in a position to demonstrate to them that those profits will be captured at a reduced risk, in all possible circumstances. And the kind of people who ski down piles of cocaine with a hooker under one arm and a Velcro clad dwarf under the other, don't generally present an image of the most intelligent, careful, prudent decision makers to the people who control the entire wealth of the world.

I wrote that last sentence knowing full well that most people won't really understand what I mean by it, because in order to do so, they need to adjust their frame of reference. When I say 'intelligent, careful and prudent', you need to imagine a new paradigm. You need to imagine the most careful, most prudent, most emotionally steady person you know, and then multiply that by 1,000. Imagine that they're also a genius, because a huge percentage of people in the industry are.

Imagine a much smarter version of Robert Duvall in the

"Apocalypse Now" beach scene with mortars going off all around him, while calmly discussing the break of the waves using computational fluid dynamics that he's calculated in his head. Imagine him scratching out the differential math in the beach sand. That's a better analogy for the actual day to day in the hedge fund world.

If you're on the quant side, (and these days there are plenty of reasons you should be) you need to be brilliant. Everyone in the quant hedge fund industry is brilliant – you can't get into it otherwise. But more than that, you need to be steady and reliable. That's the image you need to project when you're running a hedge fund, and the reality of what's going on behind the scenes should come as close to that as you can manage given your individual disposition.

But if you really want to understand what the day to day hedge fund world is like, the best analogy I can think of is this. More than anything else, the hedge fund industry, and in particular the quantitative hedge fund industry, is similar to a professional sports league for smart people.

Lots of people claim to be smart. Lots of them actually are smart. But smart is a relative term. You may call yourself a good tennis player. You can beat everyone you know. You can beat everyone at your club, or everyone at your all city league. You might even be a ranked amateur player, which would make you very good indeed. But you're still gonna get your clock cleaned in straight sets by an unknown 15-year-old Serbian kid in the first round at Wimbledon.

That's what the quant hedge fund industry is like. It's Wimbledon for smart people. And it's like that all the time, every single day.

There are no winning stories in sports. The results aren't changed because the losing team had a really good excuse. And there are no rule changes once the game has begun. At that point, you either win or lose on the field, and the numbers on the scoreboard tell the totality of the story. It's the same in trading and the hedge fund world, but the numbers are at the bottom of the page. It doesn't matter if one team or the other says they were better or smarter. All that matters, is how they did on that day.

The main reason credibility matters so much, is because in trading, just being smart isn't enough. Not anymore. When I first arrived on the JPMorgan trading floor as a quant back in 1990, being much smarter than anyone else was probably good enough on its own. I know this because that's just about all I brought to the table. I had no lofty credentials, no family connections and no friends in high places. All I had was a very sharp mind, a fanatical work ethic, and an emotionally unhealthy desire to sacrifice anything I had to, in order to prove I could be as good as anyone else, regardless of background. But things have changed since 1990. Lots of things. And they've changed in important ways.

And of course, many things haven't changed. The finance

industry is still run by people, and people are still (let's be generous) imperfect creatures. That's why credibility not intelligence is still the primary barrier to entry.

The people at every level of the investment management industry are still shallow, vain, selfish, insecure, egotistical, grasping, occasionally greedy people like the rest of us. No one, and this includes every level, especially the investors, are in it for the nobility of helping others or promoting some vaguely defined social good. They all have charities for that. Every decision they make, including what they have for lunch or what car they drive, they do to protect and increase the quantity of money.

Think of it this way. Who do you know that you would lend $20,000 dollars to? Twenty grand is a lot of money for most people. You might lend it to a family member. Since they're family, you might even lend it to them with the knowledge that you're probably never going to get it back. You might lend it to a friend from college who has some history of success. But the person you'll most likely lend that kind of money to, is someone who has a clear plan, a good track record, carefully written and legally enforceable contracts, and who doesn't really need the money from you because they can get it from anyone. It's the same paradigm in the hedge fund industry, but with more zeroes in front of the decimal.

Sure, to some people twenty grand isn't a lot of money. Maybe someone like that who had a Kennedy or a middle eastern prince as their roommate at Harvard or Eaton will start what they call a hedge fund based solely on connections. That Kennedy or middle eastern prince may start their own hedge fund with family money. That happens all the time.

But what they're doing isn't really running a hedge fund - not one that needs to be competitive anyway. With connections like those, they don't need to be smart. They also don't need to succeed. All they have to do is avoid doing anything too obviously stupid and losing a fortune. And even if they do, chances are, the person who gave them money to manage in the first place has taken that into account, and kept most of their money out of their irresponsible hands.

But for people like you or me who make up the majority of the people in the hedge fund industry, there will be no such easy road. Is that unfair? Probably, yeah. But that's the way it is, so you had better get used to it. If you're looking for fairness, go someplace else. (And when you get there send me a note because I've been looking for it too.)

OK, so there are people in the hedge fund industry who in a fair world, don't deserve to be there. Nothing is perfect – fair enough. Thanks to objective performance metrics, they're probably viewed as being at the bottom of the pack. The cutoff between a mid-sized hedge fund and a small one is probably about 1.5 Billion AUM, so that should give you a sense of scale. It's not unheard of for someone getting by exclusively on connections to grow larger than that, but it's rare.

But what about the other people? What is there to learn from the guys who didn't make it on connections? What about guys like Billionaire Bruce Kovner who drove a cab before he started trading. What about legends like Paul Tudor Jones, or Louis Bacon, or Izzie Englander? What can we learn from knowing what they know? Do they have some secret? Some special insight that got them to the top? The short answer is a qualified 'yes'. At one point or another I worked for most of those men, so you'll find some of the things that they have in common in these pages.

But don't expect too literal an instruction. After all, if following in someone else's exact footsteps were an instant path to success, then it would be a very crowded path indeed. What for instance would stop all the other people who are already in the hedge fund industry from simply doing exactly what those guys did? If something like that were going to work, at a minimum you'll be in line behind a lot of other people. And one of the things those Billionaires would be the very first to tell you is that no one gets to that level of success, by standing in any line.

Remember, your goal is credibility. What you want in the end, is to be in a position to walk into a room full of pension fund allocators and billionaire CEO's who control hundreds of billions of dollars, tell them how you're going to make them a huge profit at very little risk, and have them believe you. These guys are lied to every single day of their lives by people looking to get money from them, so they've heard it all. More, it's safe to say, than you can possibly dream up on your own. Generating sincere belief in those men and women is probably the hardest part of the job – almost harder than generating the profit itself.

Not that generating the profit is easy. And to complicate things, generating a big profit isn't really the goal – not in the hedge fund world. The goal, the actual goal, is generating a huge profit without taking on a huge risk. You might not believe that at this point, but I'll explain why it's true. And actually, for you, it's even harder than that. What you have to do is generate a huge profit without taking on a huge risk, and without doing it the same way that everyone else is doing it.

If you go buy the S&P 500 and wait 5 years to sell, you will in all likelihood generate a substantial profit. Depending on the year you start, you might do better than the hedge fund industry average. But no one is going to pay you comparatively high hedge fund fees to do something that they can do themselves for free on Robin Hood.

So how do the big guys think about it? I'm going to tell you. But explaining that is a tricky thing because the language of finance is so cryptic to the uninitiated – and the language of quantitative finance, doubly so. Any description that doesn't involve using formulas is a mish mash of repurposed words from English and Greek, all of which are very easily misunderstood unless you have a solid foundation in statistics and probability. Even if you do, thanks to fat tailed distributions, the differences get complicated very quickly and the meaning of the numbers are very easily misinterpreted.

The descriptions are also painfully circular. Everything in the markets is connected to everything else, so there is no origin point to start from that doesn't already depend on a minimal understanding of all the other parts. You try describing an elephant to a bunch of blind men who are all absolutely certain that it's really a tree or a snake. For the uninitiated, a great many of the things that people are sure they understand, all actually stand in the way of explaining how it really works to them.

Do you have any idea what a 'variable leg cash flow for a forward-forward rate' is? Do you know why I said 'forward' twice? Can you figure out what kind of instrument it refers to or how to begin to value it? If so, you're well ahead of the game, and probably have some real financial training.

If you don't know, then you should at a minimum be willing to recognize that there's a bit more to market finance than you presently understand. Being able to admit to yourself what you do and don't know, and that it might not be all you need to know, is one thing that definitely separates the successful from the unsuccessful in the hedge fund world.

I'll tell you one secret that all of those billionaires all share right now – one I know they'd happily admit if anyone had the nerve to ask them. Go ask any of them who the smartest person in their firm is. I'll bet you the 20 grand I mentioned earlier, that not one of them will say it's themselves. If they had their way, they'd never hire anyone who wasn't smarter than them. Being smarter definitely isn't the answer, and every one of them knows it. Knowing the limits of what being smarter than everyone else gives you, comes a lot closer to the right answer.

Complicating the explanation further are the industry terms which have a clear meaning in one context and a completely different meaning in another. And these can be some surprisingly common terms. What, for instance is a trader, or for that matter, what is a trade exactly? You probably think you know what both of those are, and you may be right. But in the hedge fund world, both of those words are used in a much more specific context, and can mean totally different things when speaking to different groups of people.

A journalist might call me a trader, but no one in the top tier of the hedge fund world would. In the industry, my title was Portfolio Manager or when my title was Head of Equity Trading and I was hiring Portfolio Managers, my vocation was described as Risk Manager. A Portfolio Manager doesn't trade. What they do is open or close positions. It's a guy who's working for a PM that does the actual trading, and most of the time, a computer algorithm does all the trading for him. All he really does is manage the exceptions.

Terminology errors like these aren't yours alone. The industry has a whole bunch of words - not inconsequential words mind you, but words that are central to the entire investment process - that it can't decide on literal meanings for at all.

Liquidity, for instance, is a word that's at the center of virtually every question in quant finance. Yet in an industry populated by some of the greatest mathematical minds in human history, no one can give you a mathematical definition for it.

Floor brokers describe liquidity one way, banks describe it another, the biggest hedge funds describe it in a third, and the people on the retail side have never even heard of it or don't care about it if they have. This makes those of us who try to come up with universal descriptions seem annoyingly pedantic and circular in our reasoning. If it helps, we find it as frustrating as you probably do.

But if there is a single (totally forgivable) mistake made by virtually everyone looking to break into the hedge fund industry from the outside, it's this. They vastly, radically underestimate the intelligence, determination, work ethic, insight, creativity, and courage of the competition. To people on the outside it looks like an easy job. Write some code, turn it on and poof … you're driving a Lambo. The truth of the industry is almost exactly the opposite.

When the unofficial industry motto is "We only eat what we kill", you have to believe that they take their business very seriously. When the bell rings at the end of the day, they want the money that started out in your pocket, to end up in theirs. And the leaders have a very good track record of making that happen, even though they're competing with all the same geniuses in the rest of the industry that you are.

The hedge fund industry is the deep water – the big pond. From the first moment you dip your toe, there are predators large and small in every direction, all the time. They are mostly faster than you, smarter than you, have access to far more resources, and probably know more about what you're trying to accomplish and the weaknesses of doing it that way than you've ever imagined.

But they aren't infallible. Quite the contrary. They're much smarter than average but they're much more arrogant too. They operate on assumptions which may or may not be true, and that most of them never even bother to question. They may do most of the same things right, but they also do many of the same things wrong. So, if you're capable of looking at a problem and solving it in a way that no one else has thought of, there might be room for you. Many new people break into the industry and prosper, every single year.

But if that's going to happen to you, it will take being as near to error free as you've ever imagined being, in a dozen different ways, and a little good luck besides. For people from the peasant classes like you and me, there will be very little room for even tiny mistakes, let alone more obvious ones like hookers, dwarf tossing, and huge piles of cocaine.

Don't think of this as a 'how to' book. This is more of a 'how not to' book. Having watched countless new analysts enter the market over the years, I can tell you that smart people like you tend to make the same set of mistakes in the same sort of ways, when learning to apply scientific reason to market analysis. More often than not, they tend to make them in the same order. One set of logical conclusions tends to lead to another, and then another and another and so on. From where I sit, that standard list of novice errors looks like a very well-worn path.

You may have an idea for a computer trading program that seems totally new to you, but I assure you, the odds that it's totally new to everyone else are exceptionally small. And to be really successful in the hedge fund world it's going to have to be. If it really is a golden goose idea that's profitable in all market conditions just like the ones everyone else is trying to find, then it's even less likely to be totally original. For 25 years, thousands of the smartest people in the world have been poring over this stuff, 10 hours a day, every day, using all the resources available to a 225 billion dollar a year industry and with the motive of vast riches for the person who finds it. What do you think the odds are that every single one of them missed your particular secret?

But that shouldn't discourage you. The truth is, people come up with new, consistently profitable ideas every single day. And they're able to do so because those geniuses I mentioned, all went to the same schools, and learned the same things, in the same way, from the same (mostly mediocre) people. There are assumptions in their view of the world that aren't necessarily correct, but they treat them as if they were. Identify one of them and build a system around it, and you could be in for an unimagined windfall. That's the game you're playing, and the people you're playing against.

So, this book is designed to try to save you some time. I'm going to tell you how to think about the markets in the way that some of the most successful people in the Institutional world do, in order to help you avoid wasting time on what are obviously fruitless paths. If you're going to be successful in this business, one thing you'll certainly come to despise, is wasted time. God knows the rest of us do.

But learning to think about the market the way the top institutions do will give you something else too. It will give you a few of the tools you'll need in order to present your best ideas to the people you'll need to, if you hope to manage billions of dollars. I'll tell you what to focus on and how to talk about it if you want them to believe you. Your idea may be original and ground breaking, but if you can't describe it in a manner that investors will understand, then all of its originality is wasted. Developing an understanding of how they think about these concerns should help you frame your own ideas into something that the industry will find more appealing and more credible. In institutional finance, highly credible is equal to highly successful. And though it may not seem this way to you yet, to get to the top, it's the credibility that has to come first.

Breaking In

If you want to get to Billions of dollars under management, credibility with institutional investors is your one and only goal. Nothing else matters.

Producing a higher return than others will help a great deal in establishing credibility for you, but it's not the only thing that matters, nor will it be enough on its own. There are a great many people in the hedge fund industry that produce no more than average returns decade after decade, and still manage billions of dollars, taking home tens of millions in the process. There are many other people who return 100% in a year, and never see more than 10 Million in investment. The people managing billions are able to do so because they have credibility, the people who aren't, don't.

The most common way that people produce outsized gains, particularly in program trading, is luck. But one of the biggest differences between trained institutional traders and the self-taught trader is that when that good luck arrives, the self-taught trader believes it's manifest evidence of their transcendent brilliance, while the institutional guy usually sees it for what it is. Good luck is great. It happens to everyone sometimes, and no one will ever turn their nose up at it. "Luck is a part of nine ball", as they say in the movies. But no one is going to give you billions of dollars to manage, just because you've gotten some.

If you march off right now to meet with a bunch of institutional allocators and ask them to fund your brilliant new hedge fund idea that's been performing well, luck is the first thing they'll be looking for. That will be their starting assumption. If they can't understand your ideas in a way that makes sound rational sense to them, that's what they'll assume has done it for you, and they won't invest.

They probably won't ever be able to affirmatively prove that your performance is nothing more than luck, but they don't have to. It's going to be your job to prove to them that it isn't just luck. And the only way to do that is to demonstrate a systemic causality in your trading. The biggest part of that, is explaining it to them in a way they understand and that makes best use of the rules upon which all of finance is based.

Everyone in institutional finance, or at least all the key decision makers, is an investor. Pensions and others invest in hedge funds, hedge funds invest in Portfolio managers, Portfolio Managers invest in stocks, bonds, commodities, currencies etc. They've all constructed entire business processes designed to filter and test your assertions and to expose supporting and contradictory evidence of your claims. Credibility with all of them is what you should be after. It's a small, incestuous community where things get around. And they all agree on how the rules for finance work.

This is the main reason that credibility is what you should be after. The billionaire hedge fund managers that you've heard of aren't billionaires because they're smarter than everyone else. Very few are even smarter than the people who work for them. What they are, is highly credible. They have demonstrated that they understand the problems to be solved at an institutional level, and that they know the best ways to solve them. They understand what institutions are worried about, why they're worried about it, and they have innovative solutions to address those concerns that sound to the institutions like they can be successfully executed. Your goal is to do the same.

When striving for the maximum possible degree of credibility in Institutional Finance, there are some easy things you can do, and some things which are so difficult that almost no one can do them, whatever their intelligence. They span the gap from working with an experienced lawyer for your corporate docs and working with a top tier Prime Broker for capital introduction, to dealing with and managing the limitations imposed by your own psychology and ego. You're going to have to do all of them with some degree of efficacy to get where you want to go.

I'll get to the harder tasks – this book is mostly about the harder tasks. But let's knock off the easy stuff first. I'll do my best to keep it brief.

The Back Office (aka The Easy Stuff)

Most of the easy ways to enhance your industry credibility are operational - what the industry would refer to as back office concerns. Running a hedge fund doesn't just involve trading. It also involves keeping careful track of your trades and running a business to handle tax, accounting, I.T., compliance. You'll need to deal with banks, your investors, the tax and regulatory bodies, and your partnerships with other service providers. 99% of that is considered back office concerns.

I don't mean to imply that any of these are trivial concerns, they definitely aren't. They require great attention to detail. And since the industry is so regulated, you should probably apply more care than you would in building some other business. But it isn't these issues that kill most hedge funds. Most hedge funds fail because, for a variety of reasons, they stop making a profit in the front office.

A temporarily gap in profitability isn't necessarily the same thing as no longer making a profit. Nothing works 100% of the time and there is a natural yin and yang to hedge fund profitability that the industry understands very well. That's considered the front office. So, some background info and definitions of terminology aside, the front office is what we'll spend most of our time on.

But that taken aside, you'll need to have a back office. So, the first question you'll need to address is whether you build your own back office, or join someone else's firm and use theirs.

If you decide that you'd prefer to work for someone else by joining their firm, and the firm you go to work for is credible, the minute you're hired you'll be in a position to leverage their credibility for yourself in almost all professional circumstances. The most credible firms are the big multi-strategy funds like Graham Capital or Tudor Investments. All of them are run by people with big, sometimes legendary reputations and they guard them with very great care.

Big multi-strategy hedge funds didn't get big and credible by accident. They'll have a carefully thought through filtering process designed to make sure that only the most reliable and responsible people ever get anywhere near a money management decision. So, if you do want to go to work running a strategy for a big firm, you'll have to do so by their rules.

I can summarize the rules easily, but explain why these rules are what they are will take more explanation. In summary to get a position like that, you'll need a trading strategy with a higher than average return compared to others in your space, peak drawdown below 20%, a low correlation to your market, a Sharpe ratio above the specific metric set by your employer (usually somewhere between 1 and 2), and there will be restrictions on the assets you can trade and the manner in which you can trade them, all designed to make sure you are as uncorrelated as possible to the other strategies they're already trading which compete with yours. This is all typically negotiated at hiring time.

If you go to an existing firm for a job and you have too high a drawdown, they won't hire you. I'll explain why in a bit. Go to them with a high correlation to your market, or to the other people who are already trading it, they'll see no added value in your strategy, and won't hire you. Even if you're meeting their expectations and are offered a job, you'll make less money at someone else's firm than you will by forming your own. They've gone to the trouble of building an efficient back office, and will want to be compensated by you, for saving you the trouble.

But working for an existing fund isn't all bad news. Working for someone else means you get to use their data, their infrastructure, their relationships, and they bear all the upfront and fundraising costs. Those are all problems you will no longer have to worry about.

If you have a problem with your data or with a broker there will be whole armies of people to help you make sure that a pound of flesh is extracted from those responsible. Both the time and money that it takes to get things up and running will be slashed for you. And so long as it's someone else's error standing in your way, operating your strategy will go much more smoothly. I'll circle back to all this stuff. There's a lot of other ground to cover.

The other option, working for yourself, means starting your

own fund. This will allow you more freedom to do things the way you want to do them, and a higher payout when you do. This is also a comparatively expensive route, but not beyond the reach of most successful business executives. If you decide to go this way, there are a few 'back office' choices you can make that will enhance your industry credibility in small ways.

As I said, this is the comparatively 'easy stuff', so I don't want to spend much time on it. There are a great many other people out there who will give you very sound advice on this score for free. If you prefer even more detail, then there are lots of books out there that cover it. It's not considered proprietary knowledge by any means. Lawyers will explain the legal, market data vendors will explain the data concerns etc. There are even complete YouTube channels from other managers out there that will tell you much of what you need to know. But in the interest of completeness, we should address it briefly. So, here's another summary:

You'll need good legal representation with your contracts drawn up by a specialist familiar with the byzantine rules of the hedge fund world, a master feeder structure with an offshore component for international investors, an institutional prime broker who can help make introductions to investors via their 'cap intro' team, a respectable fund administrator, and a few other key items, all carefully managed by people who are familiar with the most common pitfalls of each discipline. In my opinion, your entire accounting team can be outsourced quite effectively, at least in the early days, leaving you to focus on your principle problem, which is generating trading profits.

The fees you can charge your investors are at least in part a back-office concern and a matter of negotiation. Two and twenty (two percent of assets and 20% of profits per year) used to be the standard. But these days you can't charge that much unless you have very high credibility. As a startup hedge fund run by a first-time money manager, you won't have nearly enough. So, at the outset you should think somewhat smaller.

At the time of this writing, Paul Tudor Jones still charges something close to 2 & 20. Izzy Englander does as well. You might charge wealthy individual investors something close to that, but institutions who control the big money will have no interest in you at those rates. Offer them a deal for zero and 30 and they'll be much more receptive. The industry is only too happy to pay big for upside, so ditching the two percent "management fee" is usually better received. If it were me, I'd start at 1 & 20 and make them ask for a better deal.

If you can afford to pay for leaders in the industry for your legal, prime brokerage, and custodial services, it's a small plus to your credibility. But only in as much as it's a signal of your commitment. Also, though Legal may be 'coin operated', and be willing to work for you for the hourly billing, Prime Brokers will not. They don't see themselves as guns for hire. Thanks to the highly regulated nature of the industry, they have other more pressing concerns when choosing clients.

Most hedge funds are started by people who are sure they understand the institutional capital markets but really don't, so the failure rate is very high in the hedge fund world, and there are always unrecoverable startup costs for a broker taking on a new hedge fund client. The brokers don't want to waste time on companies that are likely to fail. Since 90% of all new hedge funds never raise more than 10 Million dollars, if you're below that level, they see your default odds of success as 9 to 1 against. Once you raise more than 10 million, their view will change.

Most of the top tier Prime Brokers will require you to be of a certain size before they'll even meet with you. Fifty million dollars used to be the lower bar, but it might be different now. Goldman, Morgan Stanley and JPMorgan are considered the leaders in the Prime Broker space, with Goldman having a slight advantage. The 'Assets under management' barrier is their primary filtering mechanism. If you reach a certain AUM then you've been successful enough to convince others that you know what you're doing. And the logic is that if you know what you're doing, you'll probably keep doing it.

I'll get into the details of the brokerage relationship a bit more later. It should be clear that apart from being just a back-office concern, it's a key relationship in the front office, and for reasons that will become obvious, it's usually the front office which manages the relationship. But at this stage, you should be aware that although Prime Brokers will go to some lengths to describe you as a partner of theirs in some areas of their business, their incentives will only ever be partially aligned with yours.

They'll be genuinely doing all they can to help you raise investment funds with one hand, while doing their level best to steal every dollar of it from you with the other 5 hands. That's actually a bit unfair of me to say. They do not steal. Absolutely nothing the brokers do as a matter of normal business is illegal – quite the contrary. No one in the industry has a greater incentive to stay strictly within the letter of the law than the banks and brokers. But from my experience with new managers, I know that people new to the industry don't typically see it that way.

We'll discuss the ethics created by those opposing incentives a bit later as well. That's another front office worry. For now, it's enough for you to know that broker behavior is the same with everyone, and you should never take it personally. Like they say in the mafia, it's just business. Getting emotional about it will only hurt you, not them. To be a bit more academic about it, In the finance industry, emotional decisions leave you open to manipulation by others, and many areas of the business are specifically designed to manipulate people's emotions. You don't want to be one of them. Action not reaction is the name of the game in the hedge fund world and getting emotional makes it more likely that you're reacting rather than acting.

Besides, the girl or guy you're dealing with on the Prime brokerage side, is in all likelihood a good person. He or she has kids, a spouse, and house with a mortgage. You may actually like him or her. Hopefully you do. Trading is a human business, and having a good personal relationship with your broker can solve far more problems than I could ever hope to describe in a single book. But the industry long ago came to accept that where interests diverge, they're diverged. And even the best relationship ends at the office door. Unless they're a blood relative, from 9:30 to 4:00 their soul belongs to someone else, however well you may get along with them.

OK, when starting your own fund, partnering with big, top tier (expensive) service providers lends you some credibility. A good top name accountant and auditor lends you some credibility.

Using Goldman Sachs 'cap intro' is better than that of a smaller firm, and if you're deemed worthy, Goldman and the other top tier firms can and will open every door in the world to you. If you're large enough, you'll be introduced to the Saudi royal family, the trillion-dollar plus Norwegian Public Pension Fund, and representatives of the Emperor of Japan. But if you're less than 100 Million AUM, it's unlikely that you'll be generating enough revenue for them to make those relationships work, so you should start with more limited ambitions.

At the entry level, Interactive Brokers has a first-rate support team for their small institutional clients and they're very inexpensive, but their custody and capital introduction services are very weak. Tier two "Introducing brokers" like BTIG, Jeffries and Cowen can get you access to a top tier custody partner which will make new institutional clients a bit easier to manage, but will be more expensive than IB, and their capital introduction team still won't match the top players. In this area, you'll get what you pay for, and the more money you manage, the more you can afford to pay. That may seem like a catch 22 but it isn't. It's a filtering mechanism, and you should plan on growing your fund in small steps.

These are mostly 'operational' concerns. Like I said, everything is connected in institutional finance so some of these topics will get more expansion in a bit. On the operational side, I'm sure you'll get the lay of the land very quickly, and even if you don't, any back-office mistakes will be less expensive than front office errors. If you can run a business, any business, you can figure out which of these service providers is best for you at the current point in your growth curve. In this regard, the hedge fund industry isn't all that different from others, and no one ever went out of business because they chose the wrong tier 2 broker or went with JPMorgan instead of Goldman.

The things you and I should focus on are the things where the hedge fund industry is not very much like other industries, and where mistakes can be so expensive as to make or break you. They can do so in ways that aren't immediately apparent.

Hedge Fund Culture

When discussing the culture of a successful hedge fund, some comparison to startups is worthwhile. Unlike in startups or venture capital, the environment where hedge funds operate is based as completely and totally on merit, as any industry run by humans ever could be. In the VC world, your relationships matter considerably more than they ever will in hedge funds. Your charismatic personality won't hurt you in trading, but it isn't going to buy you much. Few important decisions will ever be made based on how people feel about you, so there is no such thing as charming your way to success in the hedge fund world.

To be really successful you'll need some help. That means employees. Experienced employees are worth more to you. There are umpteen million tiny problems to solve in every one of the back-office disciplines, some of which can prove to be very expensive if done wrong and at some point, everyone has had to solve them. The only way anyone learns to solve them correctly is through experience.

This is important, because the people who have that experience have mostly gotten it at highly meritocratic firms. That's what their expectation will be. The closer you can get to that ideal the better quality of employee you'll attract and keep. There is a saying that staffing turnover happens everywhere and you can either build a firm where you lose your best people, or one where you lose your worst. In the hedge fund world, being closer to a pure meritocracy will attract and keep the best.

In both startups and Institutional Finance, a prestigious academic pedigree is a big help. If you have one and you've made the most of it, it will give you a level of access unavailable to others and open doors for you. But once they're open, your pedigree matters much less than delivering premium performance. If you consistently make money in the right way, you'll be taken much more seriously than anyone who broke into the industry through political connections or those obtained from their university choice.

Chelsea Clinton is an Oxford grad. At some point, she also ran a mid-sized hedge fund. No one ever imagined that she would ever deliver outperformance, and if anyone ever fought to invest with her, it had nothing whatsoever to do with her talent and more to do with obtaining access to her deeply influential parents. That's politics, not hedge funds. To reuse the elephant analogy, that isn't the elephant, it's the monkey riding on the elephant's back. Politics plays a part in institutional finance, especially at the highest levels. But for where you are and what you're trying to accomplish, for now we can ignore it. It won't really matter much to you at all until you get much closer to where you're going. If you can manage to keep politics out of the day to day, for now you'll be much better off.

In terms of internal structure, hedge fund's themselves vary so much in size and shape, that some legal and regulatory requirements aside, no one ever worries much about job titles. That doesn't mean you should use comedic job titles like some startups do. A choice like that will make you seem unserious, and will open up questions about your stability. But if you give your employee's the titles of Associate or Analyst, no one is going to care much, not even the people you give those titles to.

If you're looking for a general guide, many hedge fund job title hierarchies are structured around the investment bank model. That model goes something like Analyst or Associate, leading to a couple of levels of VP, which then leads to a few more for Director, then Managing Director, and then executive positions and C levels. This works fine in the back office, but front offices aren't nearly as hierarchical as big banks, so most cut out the middle layers and tend to go from Analyst to Portfolio Manager, directly to CEO/CIO or Chairman. In the hedge funds where I've worked the title President was a back-office role.

In terms of planning for long term growth, few hedge funds ever have more than about 400 staff. Exceptions exist, but are very rare. Beyond that level they quickly become an unwieldy management problem. Finding truly exceptional people at every level gets tricky when you need a lot of them, so it becomes a lowest common denominator problem.

Most funds with staff above 30 or so have an explicitly defined back office hierarchy that's separate from the front office. A back office Managing Director may be important in his pond, but it's the front office that makes the money and inevitably calls the shots.

The back-office handles settlement operations, accounting, financial reporting, and the portions of IT unconnected with trading decisions. If they're big enough to justify other departments like facility management and HR, they're 'back office' too. Even Investor relations is considered back office. They are all backward looking disciplines whose principal concern is managing what happened. Front office is focused exclusively on what's going to happen, and is made up of only two departments – Trading and Research, along with the key staff who support them.

In any hedge fund large enough for both, there are two totally separate decision-making hierarchies, one for back office and one for front. The back office doesn't usually need things done as quickly as the front office does, but they do need them done carefully. So, depending on the firm size, the back office may have all manner of middle managers, project managers, consultants etc. That's viewed as appropriate where the time cost for a poor decision is so low.

But honestly, no one in the industry much cares about the back office, except other back offices. If you hire this CFO or that one, so long as they're competent, it's not going to do too much for your credibility with investors one way or the other. The CFO's you interview will certainly tell you differently. They'll explain that their long-term relationships will smooth the way for you and make things easier. In truth, they may do that very thing in the back office. But the fees one offshore bank charges compared to another offshore bank should be a drop in the bucket for you. So, you should prioritize accordingly.

As a brief aside, for those of you who may want to think about a job managing money one day but don't think you're ready to go right now, promotion into a trading role from a back-office or other position virtually never happens in a hedge fund. The industry view is that the skills and disposition required to be successful in trading can't be acquired through proximity.

This logic, frustrating as it may be for the aspirational back office staffers out there, is largely correct. Every hedge fund CFO on Wall street thinks he should be running a hedge fund, but in 30 years I've yet to meet one who could last 3 days in trading. All but the most exceptional couldn't do the job for 15 minutes. They simply don't have the mindset for it.

I'm not the only one feels this way. Back in the mists of time when I interviewed for my first hedge fund job running a quant research team at Moore Capital, they literally told me so in my interview. "You will never be promoted to a trading role in this firm" is to the best of my recollection, a direct quote. Research is a front office support role. And even though I had nearly a decade of big bank institutional markets experience, for my entire tenure at Moore Capital that door was closed to me.

A few years later in a similar role at Caxton Associates, I

became what to my knowledge was the only person in the history of the Fund to ever be promoted from a research to a PM role[1]. Even though I was trained at a big bank and spent every single minute of my career in the front office, often generating trade ideas, I was still mostly stuck. And it was only through an extraordinary set of circumstances, and the unwavering support of the Chief Risk Officer and head of Quant Trading, that I ever made it to a trading role at all. Even when I did and was turning a steady profit, the CFO continued to complain about my having been promoted. Knowing him, he's probably still complaining about it today.

The upshot of all this is that hedge funds by and large, do not promote or transfer across managerial hierarchy's. It has happened, but the odds are very small. In the very few cases where they do, it's highly reliant on individual credibility that's only built up over a long period of time. So, at its best it's very, very slow. Having personally travelled that road myself, I can reliably say that there are faster and better ways to get there.

But back to management structure. Any company can be

---

[1] At that time Caxton was under completely different management team that has since retired. Different management now may very well mean different decisions. I tell the story as an example to convey a generally held view of the industry and not as some declarative statement of Caxton's current policy, about which I have no knowledge. I did have some small dealings with Andrew Law, the current chief at Caxton, during my tenure at the firm, and I find him to be as clear headed and thoughtful an investor as I've ever met. It's my unwavering opinion that he would act in every way, in the manner that is in the very best interest of his investors in all his decision making including staffing.

thought of as an engine for making business decisions, and hedge funds are no different. As a point of comparison to the back office, a well-run hedge fund's front office management structure is based entirely on ensuring that every decision made by the company, at every level, is most likely to lead to a successful outcome in the minimum required time. The people vested with decision making authority in the front office are the ones with the greatest knowledge of how to ensure that successful outcome. Merit, and merit alone is the deciding factor.

In the front office, middle management is exceptionally rare. A Portfolio Manager may have one department head or senior risk manager between him and the CEO/Founder, but no more than that. When decision making authority is concentrated in that way, a high level of trust is required, which is why so few people are promoted to a role like that without pre-existing evidence of their sound judgement. Time is also a critical component in trading decisions and front offices are designed to lower that time cost wherever possible. This is also why the banks once put all their traders in a single big room. Anything to speed the flow of information. Nothing you put in place should stand in the way of that.

Politically driven internal fiefdoms based on relationships, like you see in more traditional companies, virtually never occur in hedge funds. Not in the front office anyway. In other industries, I've seen circumstances where a persuasive head of the marketing department who might have been the CEO's college roommate, can change the design of a future product over the objections of the design team.

In the hedge fund world that never happens. The idea of an investor relations department (the hedge fund equivalent of a marketing team) deciding which markets to trade, how much to trade or in what manner, is a hysterically laughable idea. No one successful in the hedge fund industry would ever consider it. If they're the kind of people who would, they won't last long in such a streamlined and optimized industry.

In terms of more social or political priorities, if you're running your own small hedge fund and you focus management priorities on anything other than profit and decision-making excellence, it's a pretty safe bet that you're going to get something other than profit and decision-making excellence. The best internal political position for any hedge fund is no political position. You need to be focused on outcomes not intentions, and there isn't much room for dogmatic views of any stripe.

Other than scrupulous honesty, objectivity, and making every effort to minimize costs and maximize gains, there aren't any real social concerns in successful hedge funds. hedge funds can't really afford them. Unsuccessful hedge funds on the other hand, often have plenty. And though I don't know of any firms that have been outright killed because of an emphasis on racial or sexual diversity, I know many that have been hobbled by it. It's better to ignore all your own personal biases of whatever motivation, and hire only the very best people you can regardless of their demographic categories.

The biggest firms might make some pleasant-sounding noises about the latest political trend in order to keep the press off their backs, but it's only ever applied in the back office where the cost of a mistake is lower. In the front office of a successful firm, the only thing that anyone is serious about is success, and all other priorities are subordinated to that. They all know that as soon as they stop making it their absolute first concern, they're going to stop getting it.

For those who may find the idea of an emphasis on merit abhorrent, you should be aware that this also means that there isn't much room for any personal biases either. I've worked directly with people who are of every color of the rainbow, every single size, shape, gender preference, and every identity you can imagine, with people whose origins were from every continent on the planet but Antarctica. No one cared.

Two of my direct supervisors were women. Not that it mattered, they weren't there for diversity, they were there because they were the best. Since I know them both, no one will ever convince me otherwise. The very first transsexual I ever met in my somewhat sheltered life was in 1990, and she sat 4 seats away from me on the JPMorgan trading floor. No one cared. They still don't. The only thing that anyone can afford to care about, is generating a larger profit for the investors.

Though I may stand corrected, from where I sit it seems to me like the startup world loves the idea of corporate values. The hedge fund industry is entirely too competitive for a company to be managed with any top down corporate values. Only the high margin monopolies of Silicon Valley can afford things like that.

In the hedge fund world, your corporate culture needs to be centered on eliminating every error you can in the absolute minimum amount of time, and nothing else. Errors cost time, and time in the hedge fund industry, is literally money. Imposing cultural views on your employees, however high minded you may think they are, will have them worrying about something other than being the best. That will end up costing you more than it gains you.

Here's a simple counter example. Suppose you decide for reasons other than greater profit, that you should or shouldn't be trading some company's stock. Maybe you find the values of the company management so offensive to your personal sensibilities that you don't want to benefit them by buying their shares. Maybe that company CEO gave money to the wrong political party, or holds some social view that's unpopular on twitter. Let's also say that in not trading that stock, your P&L drops on average 0.01% - one basis point per day. If that decision stays in place for a year, you've just shed 2.6% from your cumulative P&L. Against just a billion dollars AUM (still a fairly small fund), that's 2.6 Million per year, a non-trivial amount in the hedge fund industry.

Add an additional 2.6% to your annual return and you will attract more investment. Your existing investors will be 2.6% happier with you. If that 2.6% means the difference between outperforming your benchmarks and underperforming them, it can have a dramatic impact on how you're viewed in the hedge fund investor marketplace. If you're the kind of person who thinks that complying with the twitter defined values of 21st century America (or any other values) is more important than an additional 2.6% of profit, then you won't go far in the hedge fund world.

Higher returns mean that all the other problems you have in a hedge fund become that much easier to solve. Lose 2.6% and they become that much harder. Trading is a game that's won or lost in inches, not miles. And every problem you address should be solved in a manner that makes the next set of problems easier, not harder. If you're going to be competitive, you don't really have any choice. If you're doing it right, then all issues will be subordinated to the singular goal of getting as much money as possible to your investors. Everything else takes a back seat to that.

I'll address this final topic again later, but it's worthy of a brief mention here as well. One of the perks of being in charge of your own company is that you get to have things the way you want them. That's great for you, but is often a problem in the hedge fund industry. At some point, every major hedge fund CEO has had to make a choice between having things the way he wants them, and having things the way they'll make the most money. It's a choice between executive preferences, and how things will work best.

You know the names of the guys who chose what works best. They're names like Kovner, Tudor-Jones, Englander, Dalio, and Simons. You don't know any of the names of the guys who chose their personal preferences, and that's not an accident. At Renaissance, the best performing hedge fund in history, the founders Jim Simons and Bob Mercer famously had completely opposing political views. But they both knew that it had to take a back seat to generating profit. Because they chose profit over ideological purity, profit is exactly what they got.

If you want your company to be something other than a machine for optimizing trading profits, even in a very small way, then I very strongly suggest that you try wanting something else. That's what those billionaires all did. Set all your personal political and social preferences aside for now. You can worry about them again when you have 5 billion under management. By then, you'll probably have enough credibility to spare whatever it may end up costing you. But it's more likely that by then you'll understand why it was such a bad idea in the first place.

The Elephant in The Room

Let's talk about the markets. The best estimate I found for complete capitalization numbers for all of the financial markets was a McKinsey study from 2009 which at that time, put the total combined value of all Capital Markets at 118 trillion, with an estimate that it would be slightly more than 200 trillion by 2010.

As I sit here in 2020, it's easily over 300 trillion dollars, probably closer to 400 trillion. And the denizens of the Institutional Finance world, of which hedge funds are a relatively small part, manage nearly every single penny of it. A pretty recent estimate for the US stock market places its total value at roughly 34 trillion – a little less than 9% of the total. At best, it's the tail of the dog – given other issues we'll get into, it's more like the bow that's been tied on the end of the tail.

Most of those assets in the market aren't the kind of thing that you'd imagine yourself trading. It includes bank deposits, all government and private debt securities including a myriad of derived instruments (both on balance sheet and off) along with all the equity holdings and derived instruments in companies both public and private. But just because you can't trade them doesn't mean they aren't all part of one thing. The rules and business practices by which they're all tied together are obvious once you learn about them.

Take this simple example. You win 1 Million dollars in the lottery. What do you do? You aren't going to spend it all on day one, so almost all of it will probably end up in a bank. The bank will have its deposits increased by 1 million dollars on that day.

It will then lend that money to others. Maybe it will be in mortgages, maybe commercial loans – there are lots of options for them. The loan loss provision for US banks, when they're actually being enforced, tends to hold them at something close to 5% of liquid assets per loan (that's liquid assets, not cash). In other words, you deposited 1 Million and they then lent out 20 Million to other people. Through the miracle of double entry bookkeeping, those loans and the deposits all appear on the bank balance sheet as assets. So, we're up to 25 million. The difference is leverage and will appear elsewhere.

One of the ways they can lend this money is by buying debt – bonds. Some bonds are more certain to be paid than others, with short term US Treasuries considered to be the most certain. They are treated by the industry and in the academic world as riskless assets. Why are they really considered riskless? That's another complicated subject. For now, it's safe to say they're riskless because the full might of the US government says they are.

If the bank buys a US Treasury, that Bond sits on their balance sheet as an asset and the cash to buy it, which is now mostly leverage, comes off. But the bond can also be leveraged. They may write swaps with other counterparties on the cash flows the bond represents, or buy other more exotic derivatives which are based on those swaps. The principle is never exchanged with a Swap, so they never make it to the balance sheet at all. Now instead of 1 million in Swaps the bank's open market position may very well have 100 million in notional cash flows. Add optionality to those cash flows and the notional number can grow exponentially.

Those cash flows are the starting point for other hedging transactions. Maybe they'll buy futures with a portion of those levered cash flows, or they'll engage in a forward contract in some other currency. Spot currency is still cash every bit as much as it was when it was US dollars, so some preliminary math excluded, they could easily lever those Yen or Euro's by as much as an additional 50 to one as well. Futures include their own leverage as a part of the fungible contract, as do options on futures, so this gives them even greater leverage.

Then they may decide that they need some equity exposure. Maybe they have a few E-Mini futures on the books in order to diversify their risk, so they want to moderate their risk further by buying some or all of the components of those indexes. Maybe they sold some Apple debt to another bank and they want to remain exposed to that specific business. The reasons can be one of many. But the actual dollars they use to buy those equities, of which they really only have to provide about half, can already be levered on their balance sheet somewhere between 20 and 50 to one.

So, taking a conservative look at it, the million dollars you deposited in the bank (that's still yours) can theoretically result in the bank buying (or selling) as much of 100 Million dollars of the equity of your choice. Instead of putting it in the bank, you could have just bought 1 million worth of Tesla stock, 2 million if it only ever goes up from where you bought it. The bank meanwhile can buy 50 Million in Tesla, maybe closer to 100 million, using that original 1 Million as collateral, all because you decided not to take any chances with your money.

Every time you make an Equity trade, you're trading it with someone else. You buy, they sell and vice versa. When you decide to buy Tesla, there is still someone, maybe at a bank with levered dollars, who can buy or sell a whole lot more of it than you can. He can buy or sell it for a wide variety of reasons. Reasons that have nothing to do with the technical indicators of Tesla, the sentiment you scraped from social media, or where the voice in your head told you the stock will be in 15 minutes.

And the bank's interests are vast. They could be increasing or decreasing exposure to Tesla because the retirement of the Japanese Prime minister is affecting the Yen rate, or increasing tension between Turkey and Greece is making the credit exposure with a particular Cyprus based bank somewhat riskier. It could be anything. It could be lots of things.

This is why most day traders fail. Because they are looking

at the tiny bow on the tail of the dog and imagining it's a decent proxy for what the whole world thinks. They make the uniquely human mistake of assuming that everyone else is thinking about the markets exactly like they are. And since they believe that the future price of Tesla is being driven by the shape of some technical chart, that must be the thing that everyone else is looking at too. In reality, the thing that's moving that stock price is the sum total of all the information everywhere, and that information is amplified in important ways by leverage.

As a pure analytic, that technical chart shape means so little to a stock price in the grand scheme, that your broker gives you software to calculate it for free when you open your account. If it had any real value, then it would be much harder for you to come by than that, and certainly no one would be giving it away free to millions of people every year. It's no more the thing that's usually driving stock prices than a flea is calling the shots on the direction of the dog.

With that said, sometimes that little bow tied to the dog's tail is exactly what matters. When all other things are equal, an analyst's upgrade or some other picayune little detail in the news really is the only thing that will affect a stock price. When those larger concerns are stable, and they are something resembling stable most of the time, then the smallest differences all start to matter. But when those larger concerns experience a change, because of relatively tiny size of the equity market, what looks like no more than a ripple in the currency, fixed income, or credit markets can become a giant tsunami of catastrophic proportions in equities.

All this highlight's one of the ways that all financial markets are all tied together. Leverage. The financial system carries a lot of leverage, and it extends into every market large and small, all the way down to the insignificantly tiny crypto markets. The banking system couldn't function without leverage. Certainly, it could never function as efficiently as it currently does.

One quick aside that I'll expand on more later. An efficient industry doesn't mean a well-managed one. You may think the banks are corrupt and acting contrary to everyone's interest, and they may well be. But that doesn't mean they aren't efficient. In this case efficiency means the rate at which they generate profits, with a single dollar of hard assets. On that metric, the banks and all the winners in the broader finance industry, are all extremely efficient.

You've (no doubt) been told that leverage is a bad thing, right? Leverage is evil. It's wrong. It's the domain of men with ill intent, who are scavengers on the body of a healthy society. Nonsense. That's just a political viewpoint amplified ad absurdum by the resentment driven professional liars who bring you the news every day, and who don't really understand anything about what leverage is and how it works.

Leverage is just a mathematical fact of life. It's neither good nor bad. It's only mismanagement of leverage that gets people in trouble. Thanks to the way risk management math is managed (or mismanaged depending on your perspective) it can get out of control quickly. But for those who know how to work with it, it's the difference between success and failure. It's the means by which the finance industry achieves its efficiency.

Here is a fact. One you'll need to appreciate to get where you're going. There are exactly zero hedge funds in the top tier, that don't employ leverage. It's the ocean in which hedge funds swim. One key to the differences between institutional investing and retail, certainly applies to how they view leverage. To institutions, any time you can borrow at one rate, say 1%, and lend at another of say 1.1%, with all other things being equal, they'll borrow as much as they can, increasing their leverage in the process, and keep the .1%. The only thing they really obsess about is figuring out when all other things are really equal.

One final thing you should appreciate is that your newly founded hedge fund is a part of a market too. Investors in hedge funds have a broad array of options, and you can think of those options – your competition – as a list of stocks. There's no exchange, but it's still a market. And part of your goal in running your own fund, is to make your fund as appealing to investors as it can be. That's much of what we'll discuss.

This is also the end of the easy stuff. Stuff that virtually any person with some prior business knowledge should be able to handle. Now on to the harder stuff.

Some Basic Terminology

Most retail investors think the goal of a hedge fund is simple. Just trade the market, make a bunch of money, and you're in. It doesn't really work like that. When it comes to your trading P&L, there is an interesting contradiction in the Institutional Financial world. Yes, you want higher returns, but not at any cost. It's easy to make 50% per year if you're willing to live with the risk of losing 150% from time to time. But that's not considered an acceptable solution for financial institutions. What they're after is higher return within a mathematically bounded risk profile.

Internal day on day risk numbers aren't typically disclosed, even to investors. But that doesn't mean that just because you're running your own fund you can dramatically change your risk profile by buying and selling whatever you want, whenever you want, and everyone will be happy to live with the consequences. What your potential institutional investors are after and what will bolster your credibility with them to its theoretical maximum, is predictability.

I'd love to be in a position to say your risk should be X if you want your return to be Y, but that's impossible. There are a wide variety of suitable options with regard to risk and return, depending on the specifics of what your investors are after. But once set and agreed to, institutional investors will want you to be consistent. They don't want any surprises – even surprises that you're sure will only improve things and are perfectly allowable under your contract terms. They want to know what chances you're going to take in order to deliver those returns.

In the spring of 2020 Paul Tudor Jones, a man who deservedly has the maximum possible credibility available to anyone alive in the investing world, decided to make a small change to his prior view, and add a tiny investment in crypto-currency to his fund's holding. To justify it, he wrote a two-page explanation of his thinking in his quarterly letter to his investors. It's available online if you'd care to read it.

How much time do you think it took him to write a 2-page addendum to his investor letter? What do you figure the rate would be, if a world famous, top of the very top billionaire was billing by the hour for the time it took him to write a two-page description of his investment choice?

Speaking more directly to the question at hand, if that's the investment that a 30-year legend in the industry is prepared to make in order to maintain his own credibility in the face of adding one tiny component to his multi-billion-dollar investment portfolio, just imagine how your investors will react if you're trading 100% equities today, 50-50 futures tomorrow, and 33-33-33 currencies the day after, without letting them know about the change.

That doesn't mean don't take chances. Zero risk and

positive return is an unachievable goal. If that's what you think you have in your strategy then I can 100% guarantee it's because you're missing something important. What institutional investors are after is controlled risk, not no risk. They fully understand that there are no outsized gains any other way. What they want you to do is to understand and control the risks you take in as mathematically precise a way as you can. And if you're going to make meaningful changes to that, they'll want a say in whether you do so or not, with their money.

Most of the people reading this will be more familiar with the equity investment space than others so let's talk about this in those terms. To understand why equity investment represents a different risk paradigm to institutions than say bonds or futures, you need to understand variance. One extremely broad description is that it's a metric to quantify the rate of change over time. More change, more variance, and more variance, more risk.

To most of you, this will be obvious. Basic literacy in statistics and probability really has become an essential part of success in the finance industry, but as I promised, I'm not going to go into the math. I will however strongly advise that if you don't have a basic understanding of what the Greeks represent as risk factors, you should get one. If It tried to explain it to you properly it would easily add 900 pages or so, and even then, I'd have to leave much of the important bits out.

This book is written with a specific audience in mind. If

you're a finance or STEM major then you probably already understand enough statistics to understand my points and if you can't, then no matter what I say, you probably aren't ready for the hedge fund industry. Alpha, Beta, Gamma, Theta, Vega, and Rho should be as clearly understood by you as a term like short sale. You don't need a complete understanding, but you definitely need the basics and enough statistics to understand how and why they're derived.

For our purposes here, it should suffice to say that no one is in any disagreement about the basics of statistics. The mathematic discipline is exceptionally well understood and can be explained in excellent detail by virtually any undergraduate math or finance professor. Statistics as a discipline is not incorrect or inconsistent in any way. The math isn't where the errors are made in finance.

So, if you don't know at least the basics about it, you should go learn that first. It's critical. And for the average reader of this book, even if you don't know anything about it, the basics won't be too difficult. But there are a few key things to think about when you try to apply those concepts to trading that will help you avoid the most common errors of an inexperienced but otherwise highly intelligent and numerate new PM.

The first thing to remember is that all the risk statistics that anyone ever generates with regard to market returns are wrong. We all know they're wrong. Believing they're correct is a frequent source of error. At best, they're backward looking estimates.

Linear statistics and probability are only ever correct with regard to phenomena described by a normal distribution. We use the phrase normal distribution as a shorthand in finance, but we all know that financial returns are not normally distributed, they're fat tailed, so everything we say about them contains a degree of error.

A fat tailed distribution means that big changes occur more often than would be possible if the data we're looking at were normally distributed. The markets demonstrate a big change WAY more often than they should if the numbers were truly random. We know this, and the Greek letters – Alpha, Beta, Gamma, Theta, Vega, and Rho, and the hedging actions inspired by them are a means of trying to cope with that error. One way you can think about it (which itself is incorrect, but is probably still useful at this point) is to think of those letters as a kind of deconstructive description of the degree of error.

When Beta is below a certain number (within 2.5 standard deviations of the mean or so is a pretty good rule of thumb) statistics produced as if the data were normally distributed will be very close to correct. When it creeps higher than that, the error term increases. At first, Beta is a pretty good descriptor on its own. Once it reaches a certain level (the 2.5 standard deviations I mentioned), Gamma begins to matter more in understanding your actual risk. As portfolio Gamma increases, Theta can matter more, and so on. So, we look at the way the data doesn't match a normal distribution, and as we see larger and larger errors in the tail events, we describe portions of that error with the various Greek labeled dimensions of risk. As I said, you should really familiarize yourself with the dynamics of it.

But the problem isn't with the math. The math is telling us what it's supposed to. The problem is with the assumptions that we people make about the what we believe the math is telling us, and the phenomena that make the data fat tailed in the first place. And all the way at the bottom of that risk deconstruction process – the remainder that can't ever be quantified and that inevitably creates all the error at every point in the chain, is liquidity.

There is no formula for calculating or predicting liquidity, because it isn't a statistical phenomenon. It's a thing created by humans, and is the product of human decision making. Changes in liquidity are a result of a group of people with similar decision-making constraints, all try to outsmart one another, and getting outsmarted in the process. It's created by the various ways that humans are alike in their decision making, and manipulated by the ways they're different.

Liquidity is the dark matter of financial risk management. At the moment anyway, it can only be quantitatively understood by looking at all the other things around it. Getting it right will make your trading career successful, and getting it very wrong will end it.

Paul Tudor Jones got it right in 87, George Soros got it right in 02, Michael Burry got it right in 08. A whole bunch of people including Lehman Brothers, Bear Stearns and Long-Term Capital Management, all got it terribly wrong. And liquidity is the reason that the risk statistics we site are only ever used as a description of the past, and can't be relied upon as predictions of the future.

That's it. That's all I have to say on it right now. We need better terminology to go any further. That basic principle is good enough for the time being. Just a little something to keep in mind as we go. What we're striving to do is to understand the myriad of ways that we are dealing with error and imprecision, and the ultimate source of those errors, is human behavior. At the bottom of those errors, the ultimate cause of them all, are changes in this concept of liquidity. And all of those changes are caused, not by randomness, or irrationality, or the gods, or animal spirits, but by people.

Allocator Expectations (And Some More Terminology)

Credibility with institutional investors is your one and only goal. It can't be over stated. It doesn't matter if it's a hiring manager at a hedge fund, or a billion-dollar pension fund looking to invest.

One of the most common questions that someone totally new to institutional trading has for those of us who may be reviewing their strategy for investment is, "What if I tell you how my system works and you steal the idea?"

Never ask this question. Just doing so makes it clear that you don't understand the hedge fund world, and it lowers your credibility with the person you're speaking to. It's an announcement by you, that from this point on in the conversation, you're most likely wasting their time.

The reason that question receives such harsh judgement is because that kind of theft never happens. Virtually everyone I know works in this industry, and I've heard of exactly zero instances of a manager stealing an idea. Not once in 30 years. I've never heard the accusations credibly made. And there is a very good reason for that. No one will be interested in stealing your idea because there is never a point in stealing something which is perceived by the industry as having no proven value. To institutions, the only thing that has any real value, are the profitable results that are a product of a fully executed trading system. Ideas can fall from the sky like rain. In some firms, they very nearly do. But without being fully executed and producing verifiable profits, there is nothing to indicate that one idea is any better than the next.

Only results matter, not plans or hopes for future results. A strategy with proven, verifiable results is considered something real, and without it, it's considered unreal. Even if you believe you've proven every aspect of your strategy, it isn't proven to the person you're talking to yet, and that's how proof works. You make an argument for your strategy. You provide evidence which supports your view. And then they decide if it's proven or not for themselves.

To be totally fair, the question of idea theft isn't solely ego driven paranoia on your part. Attempts to steal trading systems do happen occasionally, but this imaginary dynamic is the exact opposite of how it works in real life. In reality, systems aren't stolen from the little guy by the big guy. Big guys have no time for that. If they're going to implement a new trading system they have to pay someone to run it, and that person might as well be you.

The only time I've ever seen someone actually try to steal a trading system, the theft was being executed by a support staffer who was working on a system that someone else was instrumental in building. In both of the cases I've seen, it was a developer who had access to the code, thought a great deal of his own skills and knowledge, and believed he deserved to be the big guy, even dishonestly. So, he marched off to another hedge fund with a copy of the code in his pocket, trying to sell the system as his own.

If you're thinking of this path for yourself, think again. No one will want to hire you when doing so also brings a massive IP lawsuit from a well-funded and highly motivated competitor. They won't even seriously consider continuing the discussion unless you lie about its provenance, and can explain every single tiny business detail of the strategy. Those might not be perfectly clear to you if you didn't build it in the first place. Everyone who has interviewed an aspiring quant PM from another firm has seen this before. And getting hired as a PM is as much about character as know-how, probably more so. So, this isn't a road you want to go down.

I'd make a moral argument for not trying to steal someone else's system, but if you're the kind of person who would try that, you probably won't find my argument very persuasive. So instead, let me say this. You almost certainly won't get away with it.

Big successful hedge funds don't operate on the margins of legality, quite the contrary. And they understand the market way better than you do. You'll be exposed, and in the process your reputation in the industry will take a well-deserved hit. So, you should avoid trying to steal someone else's system because the risk vs reward isn't worth it if you get caught, and you probably will be.

To get back briefly to your imaginary worry, Institutional Investors think of a trading system like any other investment, and that means they think of it like a Swap - just another set of probabilities around an exchange of cash flows. If the negative cash flow of a salary, plus the costs of running the system, it's data, it's infrastructure and any of the other costs, are less than the risk adjusted return delivered by the system, less the negotiated percentage given to its operator, then they're a buyer and will make an investment.

But until the return is explained in full and validated with hard, third party data, it doesn't really exist for the allocator. Until then it's typically treated as a claim of return, and the probability of how believable you are, is going to be treated as a component of that. Allocators are lied to incredibly often, so they have no choice but to look at your claims with an element of cynicism. Until there is hard evidence, it's the industry view that there isn't really anything there to steal.

It's a simple fact that not all ideas are created equally. In some domains like academia for example, the emphasis for a new idea is on originality. If it turns out to be incorrect or impractical, that's not necessarily a negative, so long as it isn't considered derivative or unoriginal. This is very much not the case in trading. In trading, the only ideas that are worth anything are those that can be demonstrated as functional. And that functionality can only ever really be demonstrated in one way. The objective evidence of profit.

Economics is a social science and there are long standing jokes about its lack of reliability. "Economists have successfully predicted 10 of the last 5 recessions", that sort of thing. But trading is where the rubber meets the road with regard to economics and the social science of group behavior. Either a new idea produces a reliable (and third party verifiable) profit in the real world, it leads to something else which does, or it's considered useless. There are no points whatsoever for originality.

Going forward, some better clarity around how ideas are described will be very helpful to us. Applying some disciplined and categorical thinking to it right now will define some terms, so let me quote the work of one of the most clear and disciplined thinkers of the 20th century, noted economist Thomas Sowell. This quote comes from his book "Knowledge and Decisions" which I enthusiastically recommend you read in full.

Various kinds of ideas can be categorized by their relationship to the authentication process. There are ideas that have been systematically prepared for authentication (theories), ideas not derived by any systematic process (visions), ideas which couldn't survive any authentication process (illusions), ideas which exempt themselves from the authentication process (myths), ideas which have already passed the authentication process (facts) as well as ideas known to have failed – or certain to fail – such a process (falsehoods) – both mistakes, and lies.

As an idea or theory passes through the authentication process, it may be verified refuted or transformed to accommodate additional and discordant evidence. But if the authentication process is doing its job, whatever conclusions it is reaching about the idea is becoming progressively more certain. [...] Therefore, at some point in the authentication process the probability of a mistaken conclusion is reduced to the point where we can say we know this or that. Where that point is, varies from person to person so that what is knowledge to one person is merely a plausible belief to another, and only a theory to someone else. Each of us has some point – some probability level –beyond which we will say that we know something. But all things fall short of absolute certainty: life itself may be a dream and logic an illusion. Still, because we act, we must decide. And how decisively we can act depends on how well we know the consequences of our action.

These categories matter when you're talking about your strategy to investors, and maybe when you're thinking about your strategy yourself. Most of the allocators you meet won't be able to quote Thomas Sowell. They might not have even heard of him. But they absolutely will be able to tell the difference between a theory with supporting evidence, and a vision that has none. Identifying falsehood and illusion is what they're paid for.

You also should appreciate that what you think of as a fact based on your research may only be a theory to the investor you're speaking to. Depending on its origins and support, it might not even rise to that level for them. Your vision is only useful to them to the degree that they can find a way to work it into existing theory. The hedge fund industry is very much not the domain of competing visions. No one is interested in taking a flyer on a totally unproven idea. There are too many people out there trying to sell falsehoods and illusions for them to take a chance on it.

The institutional Finance industry has been applying scientific reason to the financial markets for a very long time, and they've come to some conclusions about it, which they all view as factual. If your ideas about the financial markets deviate too markedly from what they regard as the truth, it will diminish people's view of you. If you're just starting out, the ideas they rely on with the greatest confidence have been tested and proven much more fully than you or your new ideas have.

This isn't to say that you can't do things differently than the industry expects. In a certain light, quantitative finance is all about testing the limits and boundaries of the existing rules. Find a place that they're lacking, or expose a new approach that demonstrates their limits, you'll probably be in a position to make a lot of money. There is a very strong argument to be made that the best and most reliable trading strategies are those which expose a circumstance where people assume a rule applies when it actually doesn't.

Historically, the biggest errors are those which assume that the current state of things is persistent, when it isn't. The bank blowup occurred, from a front office perspective, because everyone assumed that the liquidity of the bond market would remain stable. That assumption was caused by the even larger untrue assumption that real estate markets were all local and uncorrelated. The same dynamic was true with regard to the 1987 crash, and the minicrash in 89. Errors like those, if you can identify them in advance, can be very expensive for others and very profitable for you.

But, you should also keep in mind that your goal with investors is not to win a debate, but to communicate your idea as best you can. It's not your new vision against their old one. There are no competing visions in finance. Unproven ideas, even correct ones, are treated as valueless, absent evidence. The industry's vision of the truth about the markets is solely a product of that accumulated evidence. Don't present your ideas as only being right if everyone else's ideas are wrong. That's a losing proposition for you.

Everyone that investors speak to, comes to them with what they believe are new ideas. New isn't ever a problem. In a way, it's a requirement. But it's documentation of the authentication process that's been applied to your ideas that's the primary issue of concern.

In investor conversations, your goal is to bridge a knowledge gap. Often those gaps are perfectly innocent and common. In all likelihood, the person you're speaking to has a very different background and experience in trading than you do. That experience will shape the way they think about markets and the words they use to describe their experience.

Here's an example. Because the leverage they use is measured in slightly different ways, investors from the futures markets often use terminology that's slightly different than that used in the equity markets, even though the concepts underneath them are exactly the same. Everyone is aware of these differences, but those in each market speak their own language in the day to day. There is no harm in asking for clarification and even doing your best to translate to the new terms to your standard terminology if it comes to it. You have to try to hear what they're really asking you, rather than getting stuck on the specific words or defining the right or wrong way to talk about it. Focus on the meaning underneath, not the way it's being expressed.

When it comes to your specific ideas, what the finance industry is most concerned with are theories or hypothesis, and the validation processes you're using to turn this information into actionable, tradeable knowledge. Thinking about strategy design in this way, will save you untold amounts of time, in ways I'll make clear in a bit. And successfully describing your ideas in this way, will also help you obtain and preserve the maximum amount of credibility when speaking to investors.

To the degree that you rely on the other types of ideas, you run the risk of harming your credibility. Your vision may seem to you as factual (we'll get into the limits of self-assessment later) but unless you can provide strong reasoned and carefully authenticated evidence to support your claim, you are at greater risk of stumbling over something the industry believes is a falsehood.

Falsehoods, are not all lies. By doubting you, no one is calling you a liar. Calling someone a liar is a very serious accusation in the hedge fund world where being considered dishonest can be career ending. Confusion or disagreement on the other hand, happen all the time. Having a differing opinion is no sin in institutional finance. Disputing something that others believe is a fact, like for example the law of supply and demand, still doesn't make you a liar, it simply makes you incorrect.

My point is that you can be wrong and be honest at the same time. If you do your best to speak forthrightly, the investor will probably think you're an honest person, even if they disagree with your vision. They might even like you, even if they believe you're incorrect. No one in institutional finance knows everything, and the best allocators are aware of this, even in themselves.

But if they think your strategy is based on a falsehood, regardless of its origins or their feelings about your honesty, then nothing is going to get them to invest their money with you. The key to avoiding that is to provide copious and detailed evidence to support every claim you make.

OK, so now we have some terminology defined and a bit of

the background on why it was necessary to define those terms. There really wasn't any way to go forward with the necessary clarity without it. Now that we have that, let's discuss what the markets really are, and the things that make them that way. Then maybe talking about how best to exploit them will make a bit more sense.

The Market is a Machine

All of the various capital markets can be thought of as a single big machine. All the pieces are connected. Some of the pieces are much more closely connected than others, and many of those connections are obvious to nearly everyone. A call option on the S&P index is obviously connected to the S&P Index price. A 10 Year US Note Future is clearly and closely connected to the present value of a US 10Y note. But there's also a long list of much more tenuous and counterintuitive connections that are better understood by the broader industry than you probably think.

What the machine of the financial markets does, is process information. It distills the impact of facts and events in the wider world, and turns that information into a consensus prediction about economic output. The financial markets do this completely deterministically. Though we may assume a randomness to some aspects of its behavior for the sake of simplification, it's anything but random. The financial markets are not a slot machine, they're a thermometer.

For the largest part, markets do not run on emotions. Quite the contrary. That old axiom about greed and fear may be what's driving the losers in the financial markets, but it has nothing whatsoever to do with how the winners behave. Everyone's emotions are subjective, fleeting, and not reliable means of prediction. In the markets at least, emotion lead to more frequent, and more serious errors. Aggregate emotions, lead to aggregate errors. The hedge fund graveyard is full to the brim with sentiment models. Properly understood, successful investing in the financial markets isn't gambling on feelings, it's cold, objective, engineering.

Even from that perspective, there's a clear difference between one type of engineering and another. If you're trying to design a bridge, having a wrench or spanner immediately handy will not be much help to you. Designing a bridge requires a different set of tools than you need if you're building one. It's the same with the financial markets. To make the machine work for you, you need both the right tools, and some understanding of what drives the machine in the first place.

The efficient market hypothesis states that the correct price for any financial asset at any moment, is one which takes into account all relevant information pertaining to that price up to that moment. As time creeps forward and the relevant information changes, so too do prices. This is the intellectual core of the financial industry's understanding of itself. What financial institutions are seeking to model is, which information is changing investors' minds and how much it's changing them. They then use statistical analysis to form a prediction on how that information will affect investor behavior, changing prices as a result. Behavior is what they're after, not feelings. Investor feelings don't matter, only investor action does.

Computers, programming, probability and statistics are all tools that have much appropriate use in achieving that goal. But those tools are not solutions in themselves. None of them will help you if you aren't using them in the right way or trying to make the machine do something that it isn't designed to do.

This is all a very long-winded and precise way of saying that if you aren't asking the right questions, you'll never get the right answers. To ask the right questions, you need to look at the other portion of the capital markets machine, but one that's no less connected to the rest, the people making the decisions. It's the decisions of those people which move market prices. Knowing how to price an option, or derive the cheapest to deliver treasury bond is useful. But it doesn't speak to the real question. The real question in modeling the markets is: "When a new piece of information arrives, how many minds will be changed by it, and once changed, what will their interaction in the markets look like?"

In a sentence, the true institutional goal isn't modeling the financial markets, it's modeling the behavior of people. People don't follow rules the same way that machines do, but their behavior in reaction to common stimuli does exhibit patterns. And to properly understand their behavior and the affect that behavior will have on market prices, you need to have some understanding of both the things those people have in common, and the things that differentiate them.

For the greatest part, that means looking at their incentives. The incentives across classes of investors are not identical, but to the degree they are similar with one another, the patterns in their behavior are also similar and predictable. Those incentives and the patterns of behavior that spring from them represent another deep and reliable connection between the various financial markets. And it's in this domain where the greatest opportunities usually lie.

A Domain of Rules

Market finance is controlled by rules. Not regulations, rules. Rules that impose limits on human behavior like Supply and Demand. Rules like the time value of money. Rules that shape the incentives of the various market participants, and thereby constrain their decisions. Understand those rules and you can understand the incentives created by them. Understand the incentives, you can understand, and very possible predict, the decisions of the people who are constrained by them. And if you know what someone else is going to decide, then it's easy to see how you can exploit that for gain.

There is only one way that any person ever moves market prices in one direction or the other: buying and selling. There is nothing else. That absolute truth is a manifestation of the law of supply and demand. Prices don't rise or fall by magic. They rise and fall only because more people want to buy or sell the asset at a given moment. That singular investor decision with the options of buy, sell, or wait, is the limit of our concern.

Here's another rule, one that many self-taught investors seem blind to. An individual person can be highly irrational in the myriad of decisions they make in their daily life. Some investors who finance their trading from other income, can continue to participate in the market and be completely irrational in every decision they make. They can lose money year after year, and if they're foolish or masochistic, they can keep coming back for more.

But in the institutional trading world that's very much not so. To survive in institutional trading, an investor must turn a profit. Anyone who doesn't, won't be in institutional trading for very long. And since institutions control the vast majority of the cash flowing into and out of the markets, one can make the case that if their choices are in aggregate rational, then results of their choices are rational as well. Within the constraints created by their incentives, they will only ever do things in the market that they believe are in their best interests to do.

But being purely rational doesn't mean the same thing as being omniscient. Even the most profitable strategies lose money on a single trade or in a single period, a meaningful percentage of the time. It's not about only making profitable trades, it's about moderating losses so that the average return over time is positive. It's about making sure that the capital at risk is only being put that way during moments when the probability of gain is higher than the probability of loss.

If you could freeze a moment in time across the entire universe, and then slowly and methodically tabulate the effects of every past event, as well as the location of every atom, in every electron in the brain of every investor interested in a particular stock, and come to know how that affects their decision making, you could in theory develop a 100% accurate prediction of the future trajectory of that stock's price. This is impossible of course. No one can know everything. We can't even know most things.

But that's the wrong question. The question isn't whether or not we can know everything, the question is whether we can know enough. Our benchmark for actionable knowledge is tabulating enough information about the decision making of others, to determine a reliable probability differential. If we can know that the odds of a stock rising are high enough to offset the possibility of it falling, less the range of unpredictable price change in our estimate, then we're on the right track.

But it's important to remember that what we're looking for isn't magic. It isn't animal spirits, or some obscure pattern matching in the shape of a chart. Those phenomena are ex-post proxies and estimates for other events which are the actual drivers of price change. In most cases they probably don't manifest as the drivers of any decisions at all – which is to say, they don't manifest new information. They can be thought of as low-cost corollaries at best. All other things being equal, they might manifest as a tie breaker for the corollary information they indicate. But what we're really attempting to model and understand, is the behavior of investors whose decision making is occurring, independent of those correlative indicators.

We also need to be aware that we aren't alone in this goal. Whatever strategy we're trying to employ, to the degree that other investors are trying to do exactly what we are, we need to be better in our estimation than them. We need to create what the hedge fund industry calls an information advantage. At our moment of decision, we need to have a better means of prediction than our peers. We don't need them to be wrong precisely, we're comparing aggregate behavior. But at a minimum, we need to be more right on average than they are.

In order to do so, we also need to be clear about who is likely trying to do the same things we are, and who isn't. Not all buyers and sellers are driven by the same motivations, or constrained by the same incentives. If their business models are different enough from ours, then a single piece of information may incentivize them to a totally different action than our own.

Take the example of a new piece of information like a positive news story or analyst upgrade. That new information may provide the incentive for us to buy the stock. But for someone who already holds the stock, that same news may be the signal he was looking for to sell into market strength and close his existing position.

Both investors are acting rationally to the same new information. Both investors are quite possibly correct in their assessment, and both may inevitably make a profit. But because of their existing motivations driven by their incentives, they exhibit directly opposing actions at the same time. Our decision to buy will create pressure via supply and demand to raise the stock price, while the opposing investor's decision will create downward pressure on the price. The actual direction of prices will be determined by the differential in trade sizes.

Apart from preexisting risk, another differing incentive can come from our anticipated trade duration. A high Frequency trading system focused on liquidity provisioning forms a price prediction that probably only extends 30 or 40 milliseconds into the future. If we're making a prediction about a stock price for 10 hours, or 10 days, the price change in the next 10 milliseconds represent an irrelevantly tiny percentage to us.

Even if we're looking at price data with an observation frequency of every second, they will still be making several decisions before we even have the opportunity to make one. If their decision matrix is based on exactly the same piece of information that ours is, they can be buyers, then sellers, then buyers again before we can make a single decision to act. And because of our differences in trade duration, their business model manifests to us as noise.

This phenomenon applies to all scales. If we're looking at a prediction of price for the next 10 hours, then compared to a long-term value investor who plans to hold a stock for 10 months or 10 years, our interaction in the markets probably also looks like noise. Regardless of our trade size, so long as we are making rational decisions about our execution, they'll never even notice us. The interactions of the HF liquidity provisioner probably doesn't register for them at all.

Here's another connection – another rule. The value of the
SPY ETF is closely connected to the underlying value of the stocks
that make up the S&P 500 Index. If the stocks independently vary
from the price of the ETF by an amount great enough to account
for their weighting differential and the bid offer spread,
arbitrageur's will either buy or sell the necessary assets to keep the
prices within a range of each other. If done optimally, this profit
will be captured with no forward-looking risk accumulated.

This is an important class of rule. Up to now we've only
discussed rules that are created outside the domain of relative
market prices. In the case of an option and its underlying asset, the
rule is created explicitly when the option is designed. In the case
of scaling, the rule is created in the structure that exists between
investors, the mathematical limitations of linear risk analysis, and
the fact that a market will only ever allow so many shares to be
traded over a given period of time without price impact.

The arbitrage rule wanders a bit further away from those,
and into an explicitly behavioral domain. This rule assumes that
someone will engage in a specific business decision precisely
because the market prices are in place to allow it to be executed
profitably. They don't much care what caused the prices to behave
that way. Their decision isn't caused by an external event like a
news story, but as a product of the rational behavior of the
investing public at large. Where an external event offers
justification to cause one assets price to deviate from all others, the

arbitrage rule imposes a limitation on that, and creates an incentive to drive prices back into symmetry with one another. Whether it's a buy or sell that does so is irrelevant to the arbitrageur.

There's another way to look at this same rule from the perspective of someone who, for whatever reason, is only interested in buying or selling an individual stock and who doesn't care about the arbitrage trade. In some portion, a time series analysis of an individual stock will show a statistically reliable relationship between its totally independent price, and the price of the rest of the market. Absent all other information, if the stock rallies too strongly or sells off too much, new sellers or buyers will arrive in the marketplace on the opposing side, in order to keep the price within something approximating parity range.

The quant finance industry generically describes this phenomenon, as Beta. It's an abbreviation for the statistical relationship over time, between an individual stock price, and the price of the broader market or index. But that terminology isn't a phenomenon unto itself, it's only a descriptor. The underlying causative phenomenon – the thing that actually makes the prices move, is the presence of rational incentives for an investor, and that investor's rational response to a profit motive.

By crossing the line from structural relationships to behavioral relationships, we open an important door. A door of causality that sometimes originates as the market participants analyze external information, and sometimes originates as a part of investor behavior itself.

Here's another example. Like the last straw on a camel's back, a particular news story may be a catalyst for a market crash. But the market crash itself is an independent source of information also. One which doesn't actually become a news story until long after it's already occurred. If you design a system which monitors the news to learn of a market crash, the event will be over before you know about it. So, the information that the market processes isn't all external to itself. Some of it, though by no means all of it, is purely internal. This can only be universally true if the markets are rational, and rational actors are applying price pressure to maintain relationships between asset classes.

Time rolls forward and new information arrives. That new information causes buyers and sellers to make decisions which move prices, and in those price moves, incentives which constrain the decisions of other investors will cause them to move other prices in relation to them. Those relationships may not be static or stable, but they are as persistent as the investor incentives that create them. And they will reassert themselves from time to time, as the yin and yang of new information effects the decision making of investors.

Apart from a direction, prices also have a rate of change which is independent of its direction, typically referred to with the descriptor Gamma. Sometimes when investors change their minds, buyers become sellers, and sellers become buyers. If the ratio between buyers and seller changes dramatically, so too will the speed at which prices change.

At any moment, an investor must choose between three options: Buy, Sell, And Wait. In most cases, wait will be the option for some unspecified period of time between buy and sell. But in some circumstances when market participants are particularly sensitive to new information, wait will be tossed out. If a buyer changes their mind suddenly from buy to sell or vice versa, then sometimes an imbalance between cumulative buyers and cumulative sellers can be created.

In circumstances like those, market makers who have an incentive to limit their own exposure, will begin to move prices in larger and larger portions over a shorter amount of time, accelerating the rate of price change, and giving the distribution of Gamma an asymmetric appearance. But this is a phenomenon which is directly created by the rational incentives of market makers and their efforts to react to the imbalances between buyers and sellers.

So, there are a few of the very basic rules under which markets function, and a few of the ways they're typically described. But we need to keep in mind that none of these rules or descriptions are really causal. They're nothing more than a kind of shorthand. A quick way to describe the myriad of incentives created by the necessity of profit. Beta doesn't cause a price change, it only describes it. The only thing that ever really causes a price to actually move in any direction or at any speed, is when someone makes a decision and acts upon that decision. Action matters. What people do matters. This idea either is, or should be, at the core of any successful trading strategy.

What people say, what they think, or what they say they think, matters almost not at all. Thanks to the evolutionary legacies of the human brain, half the time they probably don't even know what they think, even if they believe otherwise. It's only decisions and subsequent action that drives markets, and are the only thing that can ever be relied upon as being reflective of actual cognition. Our behavior is the one and only accurate characterization of our actual beliefs. And if we want to present a maximally credible picture of our own trading strategy to investors who already understand these rules, it's those actions that we'll use as the basis for how we describe our own choices to others.

Time Value of Money

All of the rules of finance are tied together by logic and reason, and are supported and reinforced by nearly 100 years of the very best academic thinking in Economics and Social Psychology. The evidence for the effectiveness of these rules is nothing less than the cumulative profit derived from the market by all the participants who have adhered to them. Thanks to decades of useful academic work, many of the rules that apply to markets are very clearly understood. The same law of supply and demand that causes a stock price to rise when there are more buyers than sellers can also be applied in any other area of human behavior.

Social scientists are very reluctant to call something a law unless it's been proven universally, and this is very much the case with supply and demand. There are no exceptions to it. If supply drops and demand remains constant, the price must rise to accommodate. If the opposite is true, the price must fall. As price changes, it will impose a greater cost on one side of the equation or the other, and people will change their minds about their willingness to pay it. It doesn't matter if you're talking about Ferraris or shares of stock, or the literal tea in China.

From time to time a government may try to prevent prices from changing as they otherwise would, but that will only result in a mismatch between the number of people who want something and the number of people who can get it – otherwise known as a shortage. Fix the price too low and it causes demand to exceed supply creating the shortage in the process. If prices on the other hand are allowed to rise in accordance with demand, when they do, people will make different choices, lowering demand accordingly.

The Government of Italy could, in its theoretical benevolence, declare that the maximum price of a Ferrari will be $1,000. Lots of people would be happy to pay $1,000 for a Ferrari, so "Hooray! We're all going to drive cool cars!" Except, Ferraris costs more than $1,000 to make, so there won't be any produced at that price. When the government learns this, they may order Ferrari to produce them at a loss, but that can only go on for so long as well. Before long they can't pay any of the people who know how to make Ferraris, so they leave and go make Lamborghinis instead.

There is no way for a government to jigger these rules so that there are more Ferraris per person, than there are people who want them. If I haven't said enough to convince you already then please just take my word for it, it's all been tried. It doesn't matter what the product or service is, the more ardently a government tries to limit prices, the more likely that shortages will ensue. It doesn't matter if it's Ferraris or healthcare or equities, or anything else. Scarcity is the ultimate economic rule and the law of supply and demand is the inevitable outgrowth of it.

When you look at the way the price of a stock changes, it's helpful to remember that its reflective of either a shortage or excess of supply, or a shortage or excess of demand. At the moment in question, if more people want to get it than give it up, the price rises. If more people want to get rid of it than get it, the price falls. That means that "price" is a signal. It's a window into the psychology of the people who are trading that stock, right here, and right now. This is a proven, tested, absolute rule of markets, and is true in all occasions.

The question we want to ask is why do they want to buy or sell right now? Do they want it for 10 minutes, 10 hours or 10 years? Every buyer will inevitably also be a seller. So, when is that sell most likely to occur? Has it occurred already? It may look more complicated than that, but it really isn't. Changing prices are a product of supply and demand, nothing more.

The time value of money is another very well supported rule which is at its heart, an attempt to place a value on the uncertainty of the future. If I hand you a dollar right now, it's worth exactly one dollar. You can exchange that dollar for goods or services equal to its value. But suppose instead of giving you a dollar today, I promise to give you a dollar tomorrow in exchange for the good or service today? In common parlance, you have just extended me credit. You've lent me the money to buy your stuff.

In this case it's just one day of credit so the odds of something happening between today and tomorrow to make that dollar worth less in equivalent stuff, is very small. Sure, inflation might wear away some tiny fraction of a cent, so it may only be worth 99.9999. For our purposes, we can treat that as a rounding error.

But suppose I tell you that I will pay you that dollar a year from now. Between now and a year from now, all kinds of things can change. We'd probably both be surprised if they didn't. A great many things may make the dollar I promised you, worth much less a year from now.

If, for example, I'm buying a cup of coffee, the price of coffee beans you'll need to buy in order to supply it to me could change. The cost of heating your water could rise or fall. By lending me the money you're taking on considerably more risk than if I simply paid you right now, and in all fairness, you'd probably want to be compensated for that extra risk. We call the difference interest.

I'm radically oversimplifying the dynamic here. The details in the market for credit, (what is popularly called the fixed income markets) are vast. The strategies and details you'd need in order to competitively manage a fixed income portfolio at an institutional level is at least one whole book unto itself, so I'm not going to get too deep into those weeds. For the purpose of this discussion lets simply be aware that time has a cost. More time, more cost.

Right now, you might be saying to yourself – *"Well I'm not going to trade fixed income, I'm only going to trade stocks, or options, or futures, or currencies, or crypto, so interest doesn't matter to me."*

Actually, it very much does. It's part of the rules of finance, and the aspect of it that I'm about to describe reveals a very important aspect of the psychology of institutional investing. It might not seem important to you at the moment but indulge me. When we get to the end you'll see what I mean.

Time has a cost. A cost unto itself, independent of all other costs. If you had a dollar today, you could in theory invest that dollar in a risk-free interest-bearing instrument and at some point, in the future, you'd have more than one dollar – (in theory at least) without taking on any risk at all. By the same token, a stock you buy and hold for 10 minutes is inherently less risky than the same stock held for 10 days whether you borrow the money to buy it or not. The risk associated with it is a function of time, not interest rates or borrowing costs.

Most people appreciate that the price of a stock will vary more in a 10-day period than it typically will in any 10-minute period, and if the price falls during that time, it will affect your P&L, even if you don't plan to sell it until the price returns to its previous level. If you take $1,000 dollars and you trade it for 100 shares of a stock, that stock doesn't remain worth the $1,000 you paid for it. It's only ever worth whatever you can get someone to give you for it at that moment. Time marches forward and things change. You can never go back. So, if that stock value right now is equivalent to $900, then it's worth $900, and no more. Which means at that moment, you have lost $100 even if you haven't made that loss a part of the permanent accounting record by trading the stock to someone else.

I'm sure this seems ridiculously obvious to many readers. But it's worth mentioning because it's an important difference between individual investing, and professional investing. For some self-taught investors, they believe there's a manifest difference between a realized gain or loss, and an unrealized one. In professional investing that's not so, and mark to market accounting, is the law of the land.

There was a saying in the training program at JPMorgan. "All of finance is a probability of discounted cash flows." This was an attempt to synthesize a unified field theory for all of finance. A statement so simple that it can be printed on a T-shirt, that describes all the rules in the industry. This statement comes pretty close. Central to it is this concept of time, which our unified field theory addresses as 'discounting'. Time (for us) never varies its speed, and never goes in a different direction. It's a constant. So those things that change as a function of time, are a part of our most basic understanding of the risks we're taking. And the best way to explain this most universal risk component of all financial transactions, is by looking at how a Swap works.

A plain vanilla interest rate swap consists of two sets of cash flows, each akin to the coupon payments of a bond. One set of cash flows is based on a fixed rate of interest which is agreed at the outset, and the other, based on a floating interest rate which will vary over time. One party to the swap pays one side, and the other party pays the other. There can be any number of cash flows on either side and the time periods between them can vary, but for illustration we'll keep it very simple. Let's build one swap with a single cash flow per side, both paid one year from now.

In a Swap transaction unlike a bond, the principle amount is never exchanged, only the cash flows – what would otherwise be the coupon. The answer to why the principle is never exchanged is a much more entertaining story, offered in a later chapter. And since this principal is never exchanged, the industry calls attention to this difference by naming the value differently. With a bond, the face value is the actual dollars exchanged and is referred to as principal, but with a Swap, that underlying value is just a theoretical starting point for a calculation of payments, so it's referred to as a notional amount rather than principal. The word notional is also used in common institutional parlance to include both things sometimes, but for now we can stick to the literal meaning.

Let's set our Notional amount for this extremely simple Swap example, at one million dollars. In a year, we will either be expected to pay or receive what amounts to a coupon payment, based on the interest rate at that time (the floating rate), or to pay or receive a different coupon payment based on the interest rate that we set today (the fixed rate).

In a transaction like this, the first step is to establish a fair value for the Swap, where the two corresponding cash flows are said to be of equal value right now. If the interest rate for one year from now is currently 1.2% and will vary over that year, then we can set the fixed flow interest rate at 1.2%, and the payments will be equal – at the present moment, $12,000 each. In an actual Swap transaction, there are other risks and structures that have to be valued in too, but let's ignore them for now. One concept at a time.

No cash is exchanged today. We've each agreed to make a payment to each other on a specific future date. One side will pay $12,000 and the other side will pay whatever the interest rate is on that day, against the $1,000,000 notional amount. Another way to look at this is to say that we've agreed to buy or sell a cash flow based on the future interest rate, for $12,000 paid at that time.

So, we make our agreement, and execute the Swap contract. Then time goes by and the day of maturity for the contract arrives. We know that the person paying the fixed side of the swap owes $12,000. If the interest rate over that year has fallen to 1.1, then the floating side payer only owes $11,000. The net difference of $1,000 would then be paid by whomever was responsible for the fixed payment side.

But suppose things had worked out differently. Suppose halfway through the term of the swap, one party or the other wanted to cancel the contract and net out the risk. In order to determine who pays who at that point, we need to discount the sum of the future cash flows for just 6 months instead of the full year. Let's assume also, that one month after we entered into the swap, the floating side interest rate made that move from 1.2% to 1.1%, and stayed that way until the swap ended.

We know we're only 130 trading days into a 260 trading-day year, so we can determine how much of the change in rate can be applied to each day, multiply it by the number of days, and we have our answer. On the fixed side, we have 1.2% for 130 days, and on the floating side we have 1.1% for 130 days. Apply those rates and we get a daily change on the fixed side of an unsurprising 0.6% and on the floating side of 0.55%. Apply that to our 1,000,000 Notional amount, and we get $6,000 for the fixed side, $5,500 for the floating side, and a difference of $500 is paid to whomever pays the float side and received the fixed side. Had this unwind event happened on the 49 day, the value on the fixed side would have been ((.012/260)*49)*1,000,000 or $2,261, and the floating rate side ((.011/260)*49)*1,000,000 or 2,073, with a difference of $188.

To say that I'm oversimplifying this example may be one of the great understatements of all time. Interested readers should probably throw away the entire example, and go learn some of the proper math for valuing swaps which can all be easily found online, and bears only the most limited similarity to this example. Among the many conventions I'm ignoring are day count conventions, credit exposure, some interesting math that always happens at the shortest end of the curve, and a wealth of other concerns that are all absolutely critical to correct swap valuation. But I want to make sure the single concept of the time value of money, is perfectly clear.

For our purposes, the most important aspect of the model for pricing a swap is its extreme flexibility. It's so flexible that absolutely any transaction can be applied to it with just a little adjustment. If you could only have one financial model used to calculate the fair value of any transaction, it would be a swap model. And since that's so, it can be the core of our understanding of the time value of money, and that unified field theory of finance.

"All of finance is a probability of discounted cash flows" right? We've already discussed the discounting. What about the probability? Well a probability can be applied to a cash flow in a few ways. For starters, what exactly are the odds that you'll still be in a business a year from now in order to pay us our cash flow? What are the odds you'll have the money available to do so? It's not 100%, nothing in the future is ever truly certain. But is it 99%? 85%? 50%?

And if it's not 100%, then maybe there should be some extra compensation for that additional risk. If the odds are only 90% that you're still going to be in a position to pay us a year from now, there should be a much higher payout. Valuation of that reduced probability could be easily calculated with an option model, which is specifically designed to that purpose. This means that rather than setting the rate at 1.2% we'll want either a much higher or lower rate depending on whether we're paying or receiving the fixed side. How much precisely will be something the option model tells us. The input for that option will be the odds of you having the money handy as well as the time we'll need to wait.

Or, suppose instead of a simple floating rate payment set one year in the future, you decide you'd prefer to give us the payout on an interest rate option exercised on that date, with a strike price set to that 1.2%? Now the probability of the cash flow takes on a completely different profile and may be considerably more or considerably less that the $12,000 in our initial example. Same option model, but a totally different input – a different probability. But it will still affect the way we price the other side of the swap at the outset, changing our risk profile.

On an interest rate swap, all that makes perfect sense and we can change the structure of the swap in many ways without violating the simple rules for valuation. We could for instance, have a difference in the timing of the cash flows, each with its own present value discounting. The cash flow on the 49th day would be discounted with a different number than the one on the 130th day and so on. The swap's present value would then be the sum of the discounted cash flows.

We could have 12 smaller Monthly cash flows on the fixed side versus larger annual cash flow on the floating side. We could add a combination of simple cash flows and cash flows represented by probabilities, all with their own probability values and time discounting on one side or both sides. The combinations are endless.

But here's the kicker. And it's one of the main reasons why Banks and successful hedge funds think about the financial markets very differently than self-taught investors typically do, especially in the Quant world.

Any financial markets transaction regardless of the type, the market, the security, or the details of the instrument, can be treated like a Swap for the purposes of risk valuation.

You want to buy an equity? Fine. That's a single fixed up-front cash payment (today) in exchange for a floating rate payment at the time you'll most likely want to sell. The floating rate is equal to the amount the price of the equity has changed during that time.

You're buying a put or call option? Same thing, except with a probability distribution to determine its fully discounted present value and the maximum term of its expiration date. You're buying an Index ETF? Same thing. How about a convertible bond? Well that's a set of simple Bond cash flows, plus an option to convert to stock at a set price which comes with its own probability. You're combining cash flow types but it's the same basic process for valuation. The rules never change. All of finance is a probability of discounted cash flows.

If you're a professional investor, all your company really

does is place capital at risk. That's it. That's your job. Your goal is to place that capital at risk in a manner that yields you the maximum amount of return per unit of risk. If you're a large investor or Bank, you can invest in anything, so it's important for the sake of assessing the quality of your own work, to have some mechanism where you can compare your own efforts on an 'apples to apples' basis. Thinking of all transactions as a kind of swap provides that structure. It's an infinitely flexible format through which all the laws of finance can be applied to any transaction.

In fact, the rules of swaps can be extended even further. Do you want to buy the Fiat Division of Chrysler - Fiat? Calculate the fixed costs of your payment in the form of your cash payment in dollars or stock, calculate the variable returns for the float side in the form of likely Chrysler sales, deduct the OpEx, apply the correct probabilities, and presto… you have the fair value of the deal. Any premium over that is what you're paying for goodwill and branding.

Do you want to take the subway to work instead of walking? Walking is free but the time it takes is completely predictable. The subway meanwhile costs you $2.75 whether you catch the train right away and get their sooner than you planned, or miss a train by seconds and get there later than you would have if you walked. What's the probability that the $2.75 you spend will actually benefit you in reduced time? What's the probability cost per minute of benefit? You can theoretically work out the math with a swap model.

If you think about it this way, it really starts to get into your brain. And it's like that with a great many people in institutional finance. What the institutional finance world is interested in is quantitative control, and thinking about every financial transaction conforming to a swap model definitely does give you that.

The model is so flexible, that we can apply it to any financial instrument. Add a cash flow, subtract one, place probabilities of any type around them, and the model still works. It takes into account every dimension of risk associated with any transaction. And if you're prepared to see any decision as a question of a probability, then any decision can be applied to it.

Because that's so, all Banks and all successful hedge funds, at some point in their process, think of all transactions as the sum of the probability of fully discounted cash flows. The entirety of the professional money management industry uses this basic idea as it's basis for assessment. And since they all agree that this model is flexible enough to apply to anything, it has an effect on the psychology of institutional finance as well.

Does this mean that every time you buy a stock you need to build a swap model and calculate a fair value for it? No. Though under the hood, many of the best hedge fund accounting and risk management systems do that very thing.

Most front office equity models are designed to operate at a higher level of abstraction, and let the relationship to a swap be purely implicit. The swap model doesn't necessarily give you a better means of predicting investor behavior, which in the front office is the one and only goal. But it does give you a framework for understanding if you're thinking about all the things that can happen during the predictive period.

From a psychological standpoint, I think the most important thing to take note of is that valuing a Swap is completely formulaic. There is no speculation in it. There is no place to add your hopes to the formula or the idea that came to you though some non-validated vision. How you feel about the transaction has no bearing on the math.

The structure of the decision is completely deterministic, and the only question is whether all the right probabilities are being included, and whether those that are, are being estimated correctly. There is room for error, but not falsehood. This methodology applies a means of control over every aspect of the instrument's comparative risks. And it's that perceived control which is the reason that this perspective holds such great appeal in the institutional world.

You may be wrong about the value you set for some aspect of the forward-looking risk. You may have believed interest rates would go up instead of down for any number of reasons, or that your counterparty's ability to pay would be changed in some way that would offer you an advantage. But at this moment in time – the moment of the instrument's initial valuation - it's entirely possible to apply a complete statistical framework to the understanding of each of those risks. The dimensions of those risks will always be quantities. They might not be fully understood or correctly valued, but they're all present in a purely numeric form. That, dear reader, is quantitative risk management.

Put another way, this basic swap structure expresses the perfect world of asset valuation under the Efficient Market Hypothesis. It may be imperfect in reality but in theory, it's about as close as anyone can get. It allows us to use rigid statistical methodologies for examining our thinking, and keeps us grounded in what's real and away from what isn't. No magic, no animal spirits, no correlative indicators. There is only information, how that information has been valued to the present moment, and the various wheels and cogs of the great machine of the financial markets.

From there, the only thing we have to do to use the great machine to take money out of other people's pockets and give it to us, is to be better at valuation than anyone else. When they make mistakes in estimating future probability, we make money. Understand and follow the rules, understand and apply the risks, and the great machine will do the rest. And it usually isn't just a matter of better math. Most (but not all) of the errors that people make will be some dimension of risk they've failed to include, or that they've over or underestimated, not incorrect math.

Most of those making the errors will do so because a they

don't understand that it's all just a machine or they don't see all the wheels and gears defined as by incentives and rational decision making of others. They hold some romantic vision of what's going on, or they think the markets are random irrational phenomena driven by fear and greed. They believe it's a great casino, and they can lay a bet that pays off big, like the lottery. It isn't any of those things, and those evidence free beliefs drive them to make errors. They make mistakes because they believe in magic, or luck, or hope. The institutional world doesn't deal in hope. They deal in control. They deal in understanding, predicting, and to the degree it can be, controlling risks.

Under the EMH, control has its limitations. We use mathematics that assume normal distributions to describe data which is fat tailed, not normal. Understanding and explaining this difference has attracted an almost preposterous amount of intellectual energy and effort over the last 30 years, from what can arguably be called some of the smartest humans alive. And the reason that's so is because, what the industry always craves is additional control.

Solve this problem and develop a system that reliably predicts the seemingly unpredictable events that make up the fat tails of stock returns, there will be a windfall for you that is beyond description. Since I and the rest of the industry are convinced that markets are deterministic, I believe such a solution will be found eventually. Find a way to accurately forecast liquidity changes, and the world is very much your oyster.

But in the meantime, if you are looking for the maximum possible level of credibility whatever your level of knowledge, and want your trading idea to be fully and immediately accepted by investors, or the banks and top tier of hedge funds, the way you describe it should always start with a mistake. Most often, a mistake in the valuation of some future risk. And the person making that mistake, should always be someone other than you. From then on, all you have to do is ensure that you're doing all you can to control things, and the rest is mechanics.

To the degree that they have one, that's certainly one of the hedge fund billionaire's biggest and most powerful secrets. Their secret is in exerting the maximum level of control. They know that it's the incentives and motivations of the other people in the marketplace that will constrain those people's decisions and drive them into making errors. Those errors are almost all a product of a lack of control.

They are predators who wait for others to make a mistake. They look for the limping Antelope. The mistake may be an imprudent monetary decision by a central bank, some unintended consequence of a political policy, or a retail investor who is buying Tesla when they should be selling because they think that Elon is so cool. It doesn't really matter to them. What they do to make their living, is identify other people's mistakes. And if you want to be in their shoes one day, that's what should be driving your decisions too.

Most of the money managed by hedge funds isn't invested in them, it's borrowed. As much as $4/5^{th}$ of all the assets in the hedge fund industry's open market position at any one time, comes in the form of leverage. That leverage, and the time value of money associated with it, set up another of the rules of institutional finance. But to understand how that leverage works properly, you'll also need to have a basic understanding of where and how hedge funds get the last roughly $1/5^{th}$ of their funding.

Institutional control of assets is more or less Pareto distributed. Of the institutions that invest in hedge funds, approximately the top 20% of the investors control about 80% of the dollars. But as in virtually all other things, the very, very largest hedge fund investors won't be available to you when you're just getting started.

Among those large players, BlackRock controls roughly 7.5 trillion, but it's hard to get them into a specific investor category. For you as a hedge fund, they represent both a potential investor and a competitor, regardless of how you invest. If they do invest with you, it will probably be on special terms that you won't like as compared to others. A fund like that is so big that it also has little choice but to mix their financial decision making with the political. Thinking of them as a rising nation state rather than a hedge fund investor, is probably a more useful model.

Just below them though among common hedge fund investors, are the Sovereign wealth funds. The massive Norway Government Pension Fund has well over 1 trillion dollars under management, as does the number two manager on the list, China Investment Corporation. Add lending and leverage to just those three money managers, and you get to a very large open market position. In theory, and depending on how you measure it, it could be as much as 15% of the total capitalization of all the financial markets at any given moment.

Next down as a group are the Pension Funds - names like CALPERS and FERS, then the Endowments like those at Harvard, Yale, and the University of Texas System. To get a sense of scale (the slope of the line in the Pareto distribution), at the time of this writing the Norwegian sovereign fund controls 1.3 trillion, while The Harvard Endowment has something approaching 38 Billion.

Below them in size are what's called Family Fund managers, and single-family funds. These are often the first institutional investors into new hedge funds. They're a collection of professionals whose key decision makers usually come from a background in either the big banks or the largest hedge funds, and they manage money for wealthy individuals and families who, for whatever reason, have no interest in managing their money themselves. All of these Institutions have a very similar understanding regarding how to manage investment risk.

Imagine some of the problems with trying to decide where to invest 1.3 trillion dollars. What would you buy? Apple has roughly a 2 trillion-dollar market cap so you could buy half of that, but if you tried to do it in the open market, god only knows what you'd have to pay for it. And then you would, in effect, be a subdivision of Apple, since you have now effectively outsourced your entire financial future to them.

Even if you got it at the right price, the result would be the value of your pension fund rising and falling dramatically every time a new phone model rolls out. One design change, the wrong color case, a straight edge on the side versus a curved one, and your pension could stand to lose vast amounts of money. Individuals who need that pension to live on could theoretically go hungry. That is not a risk that any pension, even the wildly mismanaged ones, are prepared to take. But even if they wanted to, they probably wouldn't be allowed to under current pension regulation.

Unlike hedge funds who are legally allowed to invest in anything they think will offer an outsized yield, pensions have very strict rules from their governments, designed to protect the people contributing the original assets. The goal of that regulation is to keep the total level of risk assumed by a pension at a lower level. (Considerably lower than those of hedge funds). Even a diversified portfolio made up exclusively of equities would be far too risky for a typical pension.

Maybe you can go the other way and avoid risky investments like Apple or the SPX altogether. Instead you can buy US government Bonds – the (arguably) least risky investment in the world. That would solve the problem of certainty to the degree it can be, but at the moment a US 30 Year Treasury Bond is paying about 3% and inflation is generally considered 4%, so in real dollar terms you'll be losing 1% per year. Hardly a windfall.

Obviously, there is a balance to be struck between those choices - an optimization - between highly certainty low-yield investments, and very uncertain potentially high-yield ones. Neither are a perfect fit. There are formulaic optimizations for managing volatility as a function of your overall risk tolerance. If you're curious, you can find the explanations from finance professors all over YouTube. The upshot is that institutions operating within such restrictions manage their optimization by diversifying their holdings across a combination of asset classes.

But there are a host of problems with too much diversity as well. If you own a tiny piece of everything, then your performance will exactly match everything and you've outsourced your financial risk again. This time you'll be subject to the yin and yang of the economic cycle and the economically nonsensical whims of political leaders. This does not suit the needs of the top tier institutional money managers. Unless you've been living in complete isolation since 2007, you may have noticed that markets sometimes fall suddenly in value. Pensions don't want to be on the downside of those markets when they do.

What the typical investors in hedge funds wants, is to be in position to make a profit in every possible scenario. If a megalomaniacal politician decides to nationalize an industry (or Blackrock decides to remove a politician who already has), they want to avoid losses. If a war breaks out, they want to avoid losses. If a dot com bubble bursts or a mortgage crisis occurs, they want to avoid losses. Pandemic, locusts, oceans turn to blood, they want to avoid losses. If an asteroid strikes the earth, they still want to avoid losses. Every scenario, means literally everything within the scope of the predictable future.

Enter the hedge fund. The industry actually gets its name not because of the manner in which they manage their investments, but the role they play as investments in the portfolios of their largest investors. To big money managers all hedge funds represent a hedge. They are a means of producing a positive income stream that is minimally or negatively correlated to the overall markets, which to them, is represented by the sum total of all their other risks.

Large Institutions typically put no more than 20% of their assets into hedge funds, and it's seen as a risk minimization investment. In the case of the top tier of institutions down to about 35 Billion AUM, they already own nearly everything in every other market that they want to. They're usually invested in a bunch of other hedge funds as well. If they're going to invest in you, they'll want you to be different than all of those. Otherwise you aren't really a hedge to them at all.

This rule for hedge funds isn't transmitted through regulation and the courts, but comes to them through market forces. No one will be investing in you unless you look like you'll help them meet their investment goals. They have a requirement for their investments, and responding to that requirement will make you seem to be a better investment to them. Their investment goals, more than anything else, are a product of what they perceive as their risks in the market. So, the same way that you won't buy a stock that you believe will go down, they won't invest in you unless you meet their specific risk criteria.

If you're going to be managing billions, you'll need to obtain institutional investment. Realistically, there isn't any other way to grow that large. And if you're going to be getting institutional investment, you'll not only need to be producing a return stream which is different than the market overall so you are actually hedging something, but one way or another, you'll also need to be producing a return stream that's different from most, if not all, of the other hedge funds.

Getting any institutional investment isn't easy. But by far the most difficult institutional investment you will ever get will be your first. But don't be mistaken. Believing that this means that institutional investors are fashion chasing lemmings like the thoughtless drones who populate the venture capital world, isn't true. Institutional investors in hedge funds are a remarkably clear-eyed bunch. As in all institutional capital markets, they think of their investments in hedge funds just like a Swap. For them it's always a question of cost side vs benefit side, and the present value discounting of the associated probabilities.

From the operational side, after your first institution has already invested, you've probably already set up your custodial infrastructure for managed accounts, you've been through the due diligence process, and you'll have ready answers for the oddball questions that come up about your background and history.

You'll have quick and easy responses to those questions you've already been asked about the financial fashion of the day. Instead of hemming and hawing your way through a discussion of risk parity controls or tail risk strategies like you'll do on the first few investor calls, you'll be Johnny on the spot with something cogent sounding that applies to your strategy, and that doesn't cost you any credibility.

Remember, institutional investors in hedge funds, are investors like the rest. They see your fund as a variable cash flow stream, and a part of the cost side of that transaction is all the time and energy they have to spend on it. If they have to spend 80 hours explaining the details of how they handle managed accounts or fussing with a Private Investigator over that one time you got arrested in college, it won't go down well with them. It adds to the costs.

But having successfully solicited your first institution, you will have learned the process. You'll have it boiled down to a minimum amount of effort for all future investors, with a personal background package that explains away any teenage indiscretions, and an established custodial process, which will only help you with your next institution. For your second investor, it will literally be cheaper in terms of a time commitment, and since you've just been through it, most of the time savings for your second institutional investor will probably be generated for them by you.

But your second institutional investor will see you differently from a front office perspective as well. It will make it easier for them to get to a yes with regard to you and your trading strategy. Every institution has a process for reviewing the strategies offered by hedge funds and PM's, but they deal with new ideas all the time, so they can never be really sure if their judgement about your process is spot on. They'll do their best to find a way to take your outside the box thinking and get it into a mental bucket that they believe they understand, but time is short for these guys, so they'll never really be certain they've got it.

But with the foreknowledge that you have already cleared the hurdles with another institutional investor whose limitations and restrictions aren't going to be too terribly different from their own, it will be easier for them to get to a yes. The next investor will approach things with a bit more confidence. Like everyone else, they have no interest in wasting time. So already having an institution invested in your fund is a big boost to your credibility.

Having a lot of big individual investors is a help too, but not in the same way. With individual investors, it's more a question of quantity than quality. If for instance, you've raised 75 million from individuals, it's seen as somewhat different than if you have 7.5 million.

But regardless, the industry knows only too well that there are a great many dim bulb rich individual investors out there, with access to lots and lots of capital. Most of them know no more about managing market risks than anyone else untrained in the process. And unless your investment came from someone who themselves has a mountain of credibility in the trading industry, even smaller institutions will provide a greater level of credibility for you than any individual.

But in order to get to a yes with that very first investor, you'll need to communicate an appreciation of the ways that market forces place demands on them. These are your customers. Knowing what your customer sees and how they think about the role you play in their investment portfolio is a big part of the job. And absolutely paramount in the discussion around those issues, is the related concerns of draw down and leverage.

Proper understanding of the institutional view of leverage and drawdown revolves around something called an ISDA agreement. ISDA stands for **International Swaps and Derivatives**

Association. A standard ISDA agreement lays out a series of capital structure and reporting requirements that a company must meet before trading in a Swap. This is a civil agreement, not a criminal one. It's a contract. And like almost everything else in the hedge fund industry, it's driven by market forces rather than statute.

One of the gazillion issues I ignored for the sake of clarity in my previous example of a Swap is suddenly important to discuss now. The aspect of a swap that ISDA is most worried about is that a Swap is a comparatively long dated, off balance sheet derivative, which contains a portion of counterpart risk. Counterpart risk literally means a risk to the changing capital structure of your trading counterparty on the other side of the swap.

If your counterparty goes out of business during the duration of a Swap, the swap could well be valued at zero, and you will lose your money. Financial institutions don't mind losing a tiny bit of money if they do something stupid. No one is infallible, and it goes with the territory. But they have absolutely no tolerance for losing money because you've done something stupid that had nothing to do with them.

So, what an ISDA agreement does, is that it lays out the rules for counterparties to trade with one another, so that the banks and other firms who trade a swap with you will know what they're getting into. It ensures enough transparency to your financial reporting and capital structure, so that they can place probabilities around the counterparty risk that you represent.

There is much minutiae here so I'm oversimplifying for brevity, but the typical ISDA agreement for the buy side specifies no more than 5 to 1 leverage overall. And since it's also assumed that you're doing all you can to achieve higher return, and are therefore using all the leverage available to you, that 5 to 1 leverage can be translated back into your overall risk profile as a maximum 20% drawdown from peak.

If you have an ISDA agreement in place (as virtually all of the largest hedge funds do), and you're using all the leverage that's available to you, that's how much you can drop from your high point in assets – 20% - an implicit assumption of 5 to 1 leverage. Lose more than that, and an ISDA agreement gives your counterparties legally enforceable options including automatic withdraw of their money, and potentially even shutting down your trading operations.

But there is another implicit assumption embedded in that requirement. The assumption is that the money you're receiving as an investment is probably already levered at 5 to 1 by the institution investing with you. So, when an institution is telling you that they require a peak drawdown of no more than 20%, what they're actually limiting is their own losses, not yours. That's how the rules of finance are imposed through market forces rather than regulation. They are investing in the hedge fund market through you, and they have a loss limit on their own investment.

This probably seems a little circular, so I'll say that again for clarity. Even if you have no intention of ever trading a Swap, the draw down limits documented in the typical ISDA agreement still matter to you, because even though you won't be trading Swaps, your investors almost certainly will be. In fact, most of the money you raise from your first institutional investors will probably already be cash that's been borrowed against other assets.

This doesn't mean you need to get yourself an ISDA agreement. As some may recall from that scene in the JPMorgan lobby during "The Big Short", small funds (especially those run by first time managers) can't typically get one anyway. Demonstrated expertise in the space is a requirement for getting one and if you're new to the business, you'll be unlikely to be able to fake it. So, unless you're already trading swaps no one will expect you to have one.

But since this limitation exists for most large investors, they'll often want some other contractual assurance from you. When you first start to speak to institutions about investing with you, many may want you to add a separate peak drawdown limit written into their investment contract as a side letter or some other structure.

Here's an example of what that may look like. They deposit funds in a managed account, which is vested in your custodial bank in their name, with you as the controlling party. You can trade the funds, but you can't withdraw or move them. Since the account is in their name, this automatically gives them daily visibility into your top line trading P&L, from which they can follow your day on day drawdown. If you exceed the agreed to limitation, since it's still their account, they can immediately remove you as the controlling party, and you lose the assets, as well as any fees garnered from them.

Other early investors may want something else called a first loss provision. Both of these requests are typical for early institutional investors who are willing to take the larger risk inherent in a newly minted hedge fund. But that doesn't mean you have to agree to everything you're offered. These agreements have a 'range of normal' and get complicated quickly, so I'd strongly suggest that you discuss them carefully with your lawyer and make sure you fully understand their consequences before you agree to one.

But back to the issue of draw down and the market imposed rules on you and your trading. If your investors have a 20% drawdown limit, that means that you have it. And knowledge of this inevitability means that there is also an informal test in place for your knowledge of the industry as well.

Approach an institution for an investment in your fledgling hedge fund with a trade history showing a larger than 20% drawdown, and the most likely outcome is that you'll fail to get their investment. In many cases they'll tell you no right out of the gate, or might not even take the meeting. By going into a meeting without a response to this concern, you've demonstrated that you don't understand the issues of leverage well enough to protect them against its potential consequences.

But let's suppose you have the end all, be all, super high performing and totally uncorrelated strategy that for some reason can only be managed with a comparatively high P&L variance. Maybe your peak draw down is some extreme negative correlation event to the market at large. Suppose also, the investor is your father in law so he's highly motivated to invest with you, and is willing to look past a key credibility shredding error like too much draw down. Market forces are still market forces. There is no ignoring them – not for you or your investors. Whatever their motivations.

In a circumstance like that, the highly motivated investor in question will simply divide your returns by a number large enough to reduce your drawdown to within their investment limits, lowering the risk you represent to them. You may look at your return and call it a 100% annualized return with a 30% drawdown. All they have to do is use slightly less leverage to invest in you, and your returns become a 66% per year gain with a 20% drawdown.

It can go further than that. Most hedge fund investors, even the really decent people (and there are many), probably won't be so kind to you. Just because they can withstand up to a 20% drawdown without immediate consequences doesn't mean they have any intention of extending the same courtesy of trust to you.

What's much more likely for a relatively new fund is, they'll want to give you even less leverage at the outset. They can always add more leverage after the fact if all your claims turn out to be true over time. You may sound like you know what you're talking about with regard to risk, but for your very first institutional investor that knowledge remains untested and unproven.

So rather than giving you a dollar for every dollar they've borrowed, they might set the drawdown limit on the dollars they invest with you at 10%. That would mean dividing your performance by an even larger number, and reducing your fully levered 100% gain and 30% drawdown to a 50% gain against a 15% drawdown. Maybe they'd go even further and call it a 25% gains versus a 7.5% draw. Your individual investor mileage may vary.

All of a sudden, where you used to outperform the hedge fund industry by a whopping 89%, to your first institutional investor you're now only outperforming the industry average by 14% per year. This is still very respectable performance and well worth the attention of any institution. But it's not exactly the legendary industry redefining windfall you imagined it was.

From the standpoint of showing yourself in the light of offering the maximum surety, and in this industry, that's always a stronger sales tactic, a better approach to early investor conversations might be to remember that your goal, as always, is maximum credibility, not maximum return.

Maybe instead of showing them a 100% return and a 30% drawdown, you should instead be the one to cut your position leverage by a factor of 4, and de-lever your own performance yourself. If you go to your new potential investor with a return of 25% and a drawdown of 7.55%, instead of sending an unwritten signal to them that you don't really understand how the industry thinks about leverage, it will at least leave the question open. It also lets your potentially greedy investor imagine that he can lever up his investment in you over time, increasing his potential gains.

If you're disheartened by the idea of downgrading your own leverage and in the process your performance, think of it this way. Which would you rather make, 100% on 10 Million, or 25% on 50 Million? In the end, you'll be paid on the dollars you return, not the percentage you return on them. And since your secondary decision-making goal is to solve today's problems in a way that makes tomorrow's problems easier, you should choose the solution that adds the most to your overall credibility.

Keep in mind, this isn't a regulation. The SEC and the CFTC have no regulations about how much less than the regulatory limit of leverage you apply to your positions and your institutional investors will have no issue with you deciding to reduce it. They're considered professionals, and the regulatory assumption is that they can take care of themselves. In the industry view, this is a guideline established purely by market forces. As such, it's viewed as a much more permanent (and reliable) requirement than any regulation. Indicate that you understand it, and on this topic at least, you're on the inside. Indicate that you don't, you're on the outside.

But if you go the other way and multiply your returns by assuming you could theoretically apply more leverage than you've actually traded, now you have raised a legal issue called fraud. You're making the incorrect assumption that the market will simply allow you to trade larger positions than you actually have without price impact, and that will not fly. At best, you'll be caught, publicly humiliated, and drummed out of the business. At worst, you'll successfully slip that past some unsuspecting family fund, and when they find out what you've been doing, you'll be going to federal prison.

If you believe you really can increase your P&L by adding leverage, then the best (and only legal) practice would be for you to add that leverage right now and prove it. You're striving for maximum return within a bounded risk profile so you should probably be using the maximum leverage you can manage, already. But until you do, never assume that it's going to work, simply because you think it will.

Back to the market forces. The myriad of hedge funds available to institutional investors are a type of market themselves. Some offer high returns, some low. Some offer more risk or less. Every bit of human creativity has been used at one time or another to slice and dice the relative risks in ways that make them more palatable to those groups most likely to invest in them. Institutional investors have a wealth of options and an equally broad number of needs.

Broadly speaking, the industry has far more confidence in market forces because they're seen as non-negotiable. They're viewed as being ultimately bounded by what's possible and what's impossible, rather than what can be negotiated or wiggled around.

But these are by no means the only requirements that will arrive for you via your investors. Among the many other market driven requirements that investors might impose, are some that are very similar to those that might be imposed on you if you went to work for another hedge fund. They're all investors after all, and are all seeking the same risk controls.

As an example, many investors may tell you that they will only want you to engage in a certain style of trading or to be vested in a certain market, because they are trying to balance their own portfolio risk between short term and long, or between equities or debt, mean reversion and momentum, or some other category. You will definitely have a greater degree of freedom running your own fund than you would if you worked directly for someone else. But the fewer degrees of freedom that you ask for early on, the easier it will be for you to solicit investment.

You'll probably be best off imposing limitations like those on yourself, the same as you should with regard to leverage and draw down. Even if your standard investment agreement and corporate docs give you ultimate discretion to do anything you like, you'll be an easier sell with some restrictions, even if they're just verbally self-imposed.

This overstates it a little, but I've had other allocators tell me that an investment contract which allows a newly minted and unproven hedge fund manager complete discretion to trade whatever he likes, is viewed akin to handing a loaded pistol to a toddler. Using a generic contract in order to avoid the limitations of the law is probably fine, but the more degrees of freedom you insist on being able to exercise, the harder it will be for you to book your first institution.

Think of it from your investor's standpoint. They're an early investor in hedge funds and are accustomed to dealing with unproven financial managers. They've built in the extra costs and effort that they'll typically need to, as well as the control structures to keep an eye on things. They believe they'll be compensated for this by the fact that newer funds tend to outperform by the most when they're smaller. As they grow larger they tend to over-diversify, lowering their overall return.

Imagine they're also a 2-Billion-dollar family fund manager who has its own clients, to whom they've offered their own level of control. Maybe they've sold their service to their investors as always adhering to a 60-40 bond to equity split, and are talking to you as a place where they can allocate a portion of their equity invested capital. During your meetings, you tell them that apart from investing in equities, you also invest in currencies– which is technically a portion of the bond allocation dimension. Maybe you also invest in crypto, which to many institutional investors, still isn't seen as a financial product at all.

(let's not get into it now... just know that it's how some of them see it.)

The next questions will revolve around whether you do this currency trading as a hedge for international equities, which they'll consider a part of risk pool A, or as straight speculation which would make it a part of risk pool B. If it's the latter, then you now represent an investment in both the equity and fixed income pools, not just pure equity. You've made it harder for them to get to a yes because of the commitment they've given their own clients.

For them, the easiest answer to give to you at this point has just become no, and they'll simply move on to someone else's fund for investment. They don't have time to fuss and fret over how you see it as all one risk pool. They don't care about your thoughts on the exciting new world of crypto. What they care about are their own clients, and their own restrictions. If they invest in you, they have an interest in being able to sell your story as well as being sold by it. To those investors it's more than one risk pool, so the discussion is over.

It's also quite important to remember that although they

control virtually 100% of all the money in the world, the number of institutional Investors who are willing to invest in a new hedge fund is finite. You can't afford too many no's. In that light you'd be much better off, especially in the early days, accepting some limitations on your discretion if it will get you to a yes. Once you reach a relevant size, you can always build a separate crypto fund, and sell it to your existing investors and others as a differentiated risk product.

From your perspective, all these requirements may seem unnecessarily restrictive. "Why can't I just trade whatever I want so long as it shows a big profit?" Fair enough, you're welcome to do so with your own money, or with investment from wealthy individuals who don't know enough about markets to tell you to do it differently.

But if you want to raise institutional money, and if you want to manage billions of dollars there's really no other way, then you'll inevitably have to live with some limitations imposed on you by investors, and by the structure of the industry. It will take a lot of individual investors to pool together the same amount of capital you could get from a single investment from the Norwegian Sovereign Wealth Fund, who is more than large enough to write you a 100-million-dollar check.

And remember, I mentioned solving each of your problems in a way that makes the next set of problems easier not harder? Operationally, those individual investors can be a huge pain. They will all want to take more of your time and want to hear from you more frequently than just a monthly or quarterly investment letter.

Rich hedge fund investors aren't known for their humility and patience, so some of them will represent a much higher maintenance and management cost to you. Some will expect to be able to tell you how to manage their money rather than leaving it to you. Inevitably it's the ones who understand the least about how market risks actually work who will be the biggest pain for you. Educating investors like those is a well-known cost in the industry. In the end, it's not worth it if you can replace them with professionals working at institutions. This is the path that virtually all successful hedge funds eventually take. In the case of Renaissance, they even chucked out all the external institutions eventually.

In my opinion, there is no harder problem to solve in any industry than fundraising, and like all sales efforts, at some level it's a numbers game. Any choice you make in any area of your business that makes that problem harder to solve will slow you down. Even in the best of circumstances where you represent a pure risk play with the right kind of numbers, and you say and do things perfectly for establishing and maintaining your credibility, at best you'll probably get a yes from no more than one investor in four.

If you make it harder on yourself in any way, instead of getting an investment from every 4th investor you speak to, maybe you'll only get an investment from every 10th investor, or every 20th. That's 20 meetings for every 5 million raised instead of 4 meetings. That's 20 rounds of due diligence, and 20 sets of data you'll need to provide.

All of those investors will have their own schedules, their own timetables, and their own priorities which might not match yours. Maybe for a few of them, it takes you two months of discussions to get to a no. Four investor meetings can happen in a week. Twenty could take as long as a year. So, the fastest way to get past the myriad of investor objections, is to not have them in the first place.

And again, it's entirely possible that the only requirement that every single institutional investor will have in common with all the others, is the ability to demonstrate that you will never exceed a 20% peak drawdown. Trying to ignore that is like trying to ignore the law of gravity.

Institutional Investors will be interested in the story you tell, but probably not as much as you think. You aren't selling a startup, you're selling a risk adjusted return, delivered from a market whose core risks your customers already understand very well. They'll really only be interested in your story, in as much as they want to test your understanding of the financial markets, and proper risk management.

Much of the conversation will be to determine the degree to which you look at investing in the way that institutions do rather than the way retail investors typically do. They'll ask pertinent, topical, legitimate questions about your investment thesis, but just underneath the surface, they'll also be judging you on this other dimension. And very few of them will make up their mind about you simply because you tell a good story.

But regardless of how strong your story is, or how knowledgeable you turn out to be, what they're actually going to want before making any investment, is proof and evidence. Part of that evidence will have to come from a third party – either an auditor or fund administrator that can validate the returns you claim to have already generated. Some of it will come from your lawyers, and your bankers regarding your corporate structure and your assets under management. But some of it, particularly concerning your drawdown, will have to come from you.

The evidence you'll be expected to provide regarding drawdown will be a validated record of your daily returns from actual trading. Not back test data (or any other kind of test data), that's viewed as fictional – or if you prefer - aspirational. A back test is the return you hope to get, and probably won't. It's too easy to cheat on back test data or to lie to yourself about its causality and stability. A great many novices never produce any data that isn't badly over fitted and will never deliver the return you hope to see in the back test. No one will ever believe back test data. Institutional investors don't give money to people based on their aspirations.

What institutional investors will want to see from you, will be something ideally approaching two years of daily returns from actual trading. That's not an absolute rule, just the ideal. With two years of data, they'll feel confident that your trading strategy spans multiple sets of market conditions, and gives them a sample size large enough to estimate all others.

As I said, less than that might be workable, but 2 years is the ideal. With less than 2 years of data, you've potentially added another layer of objections, and to some degree lowered your credibility because its absence conveys a lack of understanding of their requirements and limitations.

Even so, you might very well get by with less. Some investors, especially those who prefer to invest early, are accustomed to dealing with funds that haven't necessarily been around that long. Mentioning it right up front will probably be received well in most cases.

If you're trading now and you aren't already keeping an actual record of your daily return, you should start doing so immediately. If you can save the daily reporting from your brokerage, do that too. Validation from a third party will add a great deal of credibility to your claims regardless of the duration of the trade history. Don't expect the investor to manage the process of obtaining verification on their own, you're the one seeking investment not them. You'd be much better off putting together a package for them because it lowers their cost (in time) and minimizes another potential objection.

They'll want to see everything. Good days, bad days, all of it. What they'll be looking to do with it is to build a risk profile of the trades you make, and the capital you place at risk. Those daily numbers must be consistent (within reason) with the monthly returns you claim to have delivered. If there is some quibble about the amount of capital you're managing – maybe one investor redeemed on Tuesday, but another replaced the assets on Thursday dropping your capital under management for a short period, be sure to have that explanation handy.

If there was some settlement issue or other problem that was outside your operational control, be prepared to tell them that as well. Don't try to hide the embarrassing details. All early stage hedge funds have unanticipated problems with their banks, their brokers, and their technology.

So long as a problem can be described in full, has been solved already, and had minimal financial consequences, they'd rather hear you explain it up front than find out about it on their own. Offering the explanation for all issues in advance sets you up as forthcoming and honest. Doing so only after they've discovered a cause for concern will seem evasive, and can be fatal to the relationship.

The only expenses taken out of this trade record should be the cost of trading (interest and brokerage fees) and commissions. This is often called top line P&L, and is the only number investors are really concerned with. Any other expenses fall to you and though it effects your profitability, it doesn't affect their return. Save money by switching data vendors or by moving your office and that's great, but it does nothing for your Investor P&L. They're worried about what they will make. What you will make is secondary to them.

That risk profile data is in a sense, your primary product. It's the thing that separates you from all your other direct competition for this particular investor's dollars. This can't be overstated. They don't really care about your topline P&L number in absolute terms, they only care about your return as compared to the risks you had to take to deliver it. And institutional investors see hundreds of these profiles every year so they can tell a great deal about what you're actually doing from what it says. Far more than you will probably expect them to.

An investor with the proper experience can tell at a glance if you have a short volatility profile instead of a long volatility profile. To some that might matter, to others it might not. They can tell if your amount of leverage varies over time. They'll be able to form reasonable conclusions about all sorts of aspects of your systemic risks, which might not be apparent to you. If you made any major changes in your style of trading, they'll see it. They might not know precisely how it changed (though they might). You'll probably be surprised at how much can be learned about your results simply from combining your daily P&L distribution and associated statistics, with their independent knowledge of the markets you trade.

So, one thing your risk profile had better be, is consistent with the story you tell. If you say you're doing one thing, and your risk profile tells them another, they will simply give you their default answer, "no". More than that, they may view you as having been dishonest about it, and that is NOT a reputation you want to see grow. Your best and most useful assumption will be that you are not smart enough to fool them in any way. In truth you may be, but you probably aren't. And if you get caught distorting or misrepresenting the facts, even once, word will inevitably get around.

If you don't present a fully consistent picture or if anything looks or sounds fishy to them, when they're having a beer with their friend from another allocator one night and your name comes up, they'll say "Oh yeah, I looked at those guys, but their story and their returns didn't match up so we passed. There might be something dodgy there, you had better look at those guys carefully." Without any direct interaction, you just lost another investor. Conversations like that happen, every single day.

This is a bit of an aside, but it's relevant. There's another key difference between the hedge fund world and other industries. In a certain respect, everything you do in the investment industry is public, even things you may currently see as purely internal management decisions. Support staff like analysts and programmers move from firm to firm all the time. Everyone talks to everyone else in the industry, so if you hire or fire someone for reasons other than job performance, the industry will eventually hear about it.

Put your illiterate brother in law in a critical position of responsibility, and everyone will know. Let your CFO make what should be front office decisions, it will get out. Come across as even marginally dishonest to anyone above you or below even internally, and that reputation may follow you. There is no hiding in the hedge fund world, or really anywhere in institutional finance. It's a closed, deeply incestuous community where everyone whose opinions will matter to you is no more than 2 degrees of separation away from everyone else. Your reputation and the credibility that goes with it, are in many respects, your life's blood.

You can still be idiosyncratic and quirky, but not so much that it would make anyone question your goals. Those goals, properly identified, are that every single managerial decision you make and every aspect of how you build and run your business is designed for no purpose other than to deliver the maximum profit to your investors. If you're guarding your industry credibility like you should, the best solution is not to make any choices in any area of your business for any other reason, because it will always come back to you.

So, when you're thinking about how to present yourself and your strategy to investors and really to everyone, there is one absolutely critical thing to remember. You cannot, under any circumstances, lie. You'll be found out, and having been once exposed, at a minimum, you've seen your very last institutional investment. Getting caught in a lie by an investor is very bad, but even worse would be getting away with a lie. Bernie Madoff lied. In my opinion, Jon Corzine lied. The institutional financial industry is still dealing with the repercussions of their success at lying. You do not want anyone to think of you and them as being similar in any way.

You don't even want there to be any serious questions about whether or not you're lying. Being branded as dishonest is professional death in the hedge fund world. This may seem ironic to you given the reputation of the hedge fund industry enjoys in the media and entertainment industries. In those industries, lying is the order of the day so they're just projecting their own industry ethics onto the hedge fund world. But I assure you in the top tier of the hedge fund industry your future is completely dependent on being seen as honest. Have anyone with their own industry credibility call you a liar, and to the degree that they are believed themselves, your future in the industry is over.

There is a great deal of confusion lately about what constitutes a lie, so for the purpose of clarity, let me expand a bit. You can say that you believe the market is going to rise 1,000 points and be mistaken. No one will call you a liar. The future is uncertain. Everyone in the industry knows that, and you're only stating your belief. You can say that you're moving your office to Park Avenue and then cancel your plans later, and no one will call you a liar because it doesn't affect investor return or risk. New information arrived and you changed your mind.

There can be all sorts of misunderstandings that don't qualify as lies. In an industry where there is no absolute definition of a whole bunch of the central terminology, misunderstandings are all but unavoidable. I don't think it's possible to get on boarded with a prime broker without one or two misunderstandings. None of that qualifies as lies.

You can even have a dispute with an individual investor. Wealthy individuals are not institutions, not even when they control a similar amount of money. Wealthy individuals, particularly those from industries other than the capital markets, have a reputation for being entitled, extremely demanding, and understanding about 30% of what they think they do. Misunderstandings do occur, and everyone is aware of that. If the investor is rich enough, they probably have their own reputation in the industry for being overly entitled and slightly crazy. I can give you the names of quite a few who probably meet that description.

But claim that you delivered 28% return to investors while only delivering 17%, and your career is over. If an investor believed 28%, invested, then found out later is was really only 17%, you're probably going to be sued. If they lost money in the process, you may be going to jail. No one will care that you're still doing better than the average. Claim that you never sell uncovered option premium only to have it appear in your trade record, (and it will be pretty plainly visible to those of us with the experience to look for it) and you'll have a lot of explaining to do at a minimum. Even assuming you can explain it, there's probably going to be some financial consequences for you.

I even once saw a man's career end at a big fund simply because he energetically insisted that he fully understood a risk management concept that he obviously didn't. He had to insist very vigorously in order to convince the people involved that it wasn't simply a misunderstanding and was in fact a lie. They were trying very hard to give him the benefit of the doubt. Had he simply admitted his ignorance and agreed to end the practice being discussed, I think all would have been forgiven. But his pride and ego got in the way and he insisted that he was right, so it ended his entire career in finance instead. I think he's a golf pro now.

No one knows everything, and no one will expect it of you. "I don't know" is a perfectly good response much of the time when speaking to allocators. Asking for clarification when something is asked of you, is always seen as acceptable. But be very careful about saying one thing when you know the truth to be another.

Even stretching the truth like many do in the Venture Capital world is considered extremely risky, and you should avoid it. Saying you have an operational problem solved already when all you really have is the plan to solve it later, is not something a hedge fund can afford to do. An extreme example of this from the Startup world would be the Theranos story, and allegations against Elizabeth Holmes, but it's a public secret that a large number of startup CEO's do a similar thing on a smaller scale. They have time between transactions to address their problems. You don't.

You'll be investing tomorrow. What matters to your investors are the risks you take and the returns you deliver against them tomorrow. Your institutional investors will probably see that return the following day. A future solution is not going to help you, and if you present one as an accomplished fact when it isn't, that can do you great harm. Probably much greater damage than the problem itself. If those allegations are true and Elizabeth Holmes was in the hedge fund industry, she'd have gone to prison ages ago.

Mistakes happen. Everyone in the industry knows that. The industry even has a discipline dedicated to addressing it called (appropriately enough) exception management. Errors by themselves won't put your reputation at risk, but lying about them might.

So long as the mistake was made in spite of appropriate managerial controls, and was responded to in a thoughtful way with a resolution that reflects a minimum cost, most mistakes will be understood and forgiven, most of the time, especially when you're new. They might even forgive you if the error caused you to lose a bit of their money. But develop a reputation as someone who is even the slightest bit shady, sketchy or dodgy with the truth, and you will never, ever get to the top tier of the hedge fund industry, where the really big money is.

I've seen several people stumble on this issue over the years. People who, in other circumstances I would describe as basically honest. But between the pressure and what they saw as the potential consequences, they believed they could get away with stretching the truth just a bit. "Spin" is no doubt a word that went through each of their minds. They were usually concerned that their error made them seem dangerously ignorant, and that ignorance made them likewise seem like a bad investment. I can't say this strongly enough, being seen as ignorant in institutional investing, is infinitely better than being seen as dishonest, so less spin rather than more, should be your starting point.

Even with a minimum spin you're already in exceptionally dangerous territory. Going from trusted to untrusted is not something that most people can bounce back from in the hedge fund world. It's certainly more than any first-year manager can afford.

I've mentioned the idea of market efficiency a few times, and it's important to have a clear idea of what this means in terms of market behavior.

Suppose instead of being a Monopoly, there were a thousand Facebooks, all selling the exact same product – your demographic and online browsing data, to advertisers. Suppose too, that they were all forced to pay you for the use of your data. For the purpose of this discussion, let's assume that each of these Facebooks would collect a dollar in ad revenue, and a portion of that money determined by them, would flow through to the person who is, in theory, consuming those ads.

They would all be just as interested in locking in a share of that market as the actual Facebook is, so they would no doubt specialize and focus on what they're best at. For this discussion, let's just ignore the tech issues and assume that they would also be able to work together seamlessly to give you the ability to communicate and connect with your friends and other social groupings that you're interested in. (If you're of a more free-market imagination, imagine Facebook itself was broken into 1,000 different marketing companies, all operating on the same basic utility based communications infrastructure.)

Some of these companies might specialize in certain

geographies, paying you slightly more than others when you entered or left them. Los Angeles, for instance, or the city of New York. Some might be expert in understanding what people are likely to buy while traveling on vacation, and pay you slightly more for your data depending on whether you took an airplane to get where you are, or maybe on how far you were from your home.

Others still might be expert in tracking and managing your data on a calendar basis, paying you more certain days of the month than others. There's no end to the theoretical specializations, but it would all be based on results. Those specializations that produced greater profit for advertisers in the form of more sales per dollar spent, would generate and share greater revenue. Advertisers are only too willing to spend more for ads through a channel that's statistically more likely to produce actual sales, which is their inevitable goal.

Let's imagine a world where this process has gone on for a while, and the various companies have processed all our information with a stunning level of effectiveness. Suppose it went so far, that there were companies competing in each particular specialty, but were doing so with different management philosophies that lowered their individual operating cost.

Say one company was using extensive (but expensive) industry experts while another was using AI or machine learning. Where one company could charge an advertiser one dollar for a certain unit of advertising, returning them 3% in sales, and giving

10 cents to the owner of the data, due to their lower operating costs others may only be charging only eighty cents for similar access, and delivering 2.996% in sales, while giving the same 10 cents to the user. Some cash strapped or low margin ad buyers might find the 20% savings in cost versus the .004% loss in sales very appealing while others might not.

Let's go even further. Suppose that circumstance has been in place for a while with the costs to the advertiser per unit of sales falling like a stone, and the pay to the user for their data, steadily increasing. The next tier of increased efficiency would probably be the user optimizers.

Sooner or later someone would write an App – probably run by an AI – which would track and manage your individual information and give you access to your social media through the whichever marketing company will offer you the maximum payout per unit. This wouldn't necessarily increase the value to the ad buyer, but it would for the consumer. And they'd get an increasingly large portion of the sales while the men in the middle are squeezed.

Others might do some careful math and determine that it's better for most users to be paid the same higher rate all the time, but they would then resell their data to an optimizing channel on their own, while redirecting all their social access through a single portal.

Over time, the advertisers will pay as little as possible for generating the maximum sales possible, the user will get as much as is possible for the use of their data, and the profit per unit of user data for the middlemen will be squeezed down to its theoretical minimum.

This is what it looks like when a market gains in efficiency. More final sales revenue is generated for each Ad dollar spent while the actual commodity, the user's data, is assigned a higher, and higher value. Or to say that another way, the price of the Ad is becoming a more and more accurate reflection of the actual value in sales that it delivers. And since that price is more accurate at any moment, both the buyer and the seller of the data can benefit in their own way.

What I'm describing here is an actual marketplace that already exists – the online advertising marketplace. It may not have an exchange or traders (though my understanding is that there are companies out there who are trying to remedy that), but it's still a market. At the limit of the principle, everywhere that people compete freely to deliver value to an array of consumers with differing desires, what arises to meet the need constitutes a market.

I'm imagining this one with a slightly different set of rules than the ones in place today, where the actual commodity being bought and sold – user data – has both a buyer and a seller, instead of it being given away for free. But that doesn't change the nature of the market. All that does is increase the incentives for innovation, and the speed at which new innovations will occur.

The ad market such as it is, is already undergoing exactly this kind of increase in efficiency, albeit only on the buyer side. But as you can see from this description, it's still a comparatively inefficient market compared to the capital markets, so the benefit to a person who comes up with a way to increase its efficiency in even a comparatively small way, stands to benefit greatly. They also won't have too many people competing against them for the new efficiency that their improvement identifies.

If you could statistically prove that any advertiser that uses your optimization algorithm for managing it's Facebook ads would achieve a .01% increase in sales, it would represent hundreds of millions of dollars in increased ad spending efficiency per year. It might take some genuine selling effort to get up and running, but once your industry credibility reached a certain threshold, the world would beat a path to your door. This is what a low efficiency market looks like while it's rapidly increasing.

The important aspect that we should keep in mind is that any inefficiency in the market is captured by a company. Once they capture it, that dollar of ad revenue is no longer available to their competition to capture. If one group or another of ad viewers' behavior can be estimated more accurately, and that results in greater actual sales, then because the company has already accessed it, it goes away. The market becomes more efficient, and the cost of an Ad is a more and more accurate reflection of user's actual behavior with regard to the ads.

For comparison, let's look at a market on the other end of the market efficiency spectrum. Let's look at the market for US Equities. Compared to the Ad market it's huge in comparison and is much more efficient already. There are already many more players seeking out new inefficiencies, and finding an untapped one is a bit more difficult, but when found it's often more lucrative in dollar terms because of the size of the market.

Right now, today, any individual investor can buy or sell a share in a US stock for free. Their buying and selling data – their orders - will be routed to a high frequency market maker who will capture as much as 40% (in aggregate) of the bid-offer difference in price at the time of the order. From this effort, the market maker gets a variable profit, the retail broker who sold them their data gets a fixed fee, and the retail client, pays no visible cost at all.

Every institution involved in this process, has made a trade that looks to them like a swap. The retail broker has traded away the variable revenue that might have been generated by charging their customers direct commission, in exchange for the fixed payout from the High Frequency firm. As a kicker, they also get a probability of more rapid growth which comes from selling their service to their customers at zero commissions, substantially underbidding their higher commission competition. They bought the fixed side from the HF market maker, and sold the floating side to the client who no longer pays anything directly.

The High Frequency market maker has traded away the fixed fee they pay to the broker for their order flow data. From this, they generate a knowledge gap between themselves and their direct competitors in the high frequency space regarding what is about to happen to the supply and demand for stocks. Their profit from this knowledge gap is variable, but thanks to a highly efficient business model, it's considerably greater than the fixed fee they pay to the online broker to get the data. They have sold the fixed side to the broker, and bought the floating side from the market.

And finally, the investor gets a fee of zero instead of some positive number every time they trade, but they pay for everything else in the form of a somewhat worse execution at the time of their order. But here's the critical issue. Yes, they're giving the HF market maker a tiny profit per trade, but they aren't paying all of it.

For starters, aggregate pricing smooths over the retail trader's costs, giving an advantage to the largest market participants who are trading the most frequently. But more important, the HF market maker is establishing an information advantage over their peers. A portion of the total profit flowing to the HF firm who buys the order data is being paid by the other market participants in that stock, whichever broker they use. An information advantage when properly applied, is an advantage over everyone, so a portion of what used to be a retail commission is now being paid by some other investor entirely. Which investor? The one making the least efficient and least rational decision.

In theory at least, it's entirely possible that everyone benefits from the increased efficiency of the overall market. They all benefit because the actual price being paid at any particular moment is a better reflection of a fair price, thanks to the new information being included in pricing by the HF market maker. After their transaction takes place, stock prices include the knowledge of the presence of those no commission orders, incorporated into current price by the market makers who act with that improved knowledge.

Since the retail investors are trading commission free, it's not difficult to imagine that more trading is occurring than otherwise would have, so there are more orders in the market overall, and more overall liquidity available. That means other investors will be slightly more likely to be able to buy and sell the number of shares they want, when they want to buy and sell them. This means that so long as the individuals involved are all making rational decisions, it's entirely likely that everyone wins. The only people who are paying more are those making irrational decisions, or those with comparatively inefficient decision-making models.

There are other examples of this kind of trade across the spectrum of the industry. If for instance, the investor can't afford a full share of stock, other parties will sell them a fungible swap which represents a partial interest in a single share. The company will take on the floating risk in exposure for the remaining partial shares they'd be forced to hold in inventory in order to provide this service, in exchange for the order data generated, which they will in turn sell to a HF market maker in the manner above. They keep the positive fixed revenue, and manage the floating side by making use of their information advantage at a scale of all their customers.

If the investor isn't sure which stock to buy and would prefer to expose themselves to the risk in the broader market, there are other parties who will allow them to buy an interest in a company that does so for them – an index ETF. Their profit will come from the differential risk in arbitraging the ETF member stocks with their total dollars of capitalization in the ETF. They have greater visibility into the demand side of their ETF, so they too have an information advantage in the arbitrage. They pay the fixed, and buy the float.

Other still will use their low comparative interest rate to offer that same service available on a levered basis. You buy one stake in an ETF and they give you two shares – the second one bought by the company managing the ETF with levered dollars. Their exposure to the ETF constituents is doubled, but so too is the volatility of the difference in price between that and the ETF they sold to their investor, so apart from some degradation due to the time value of money, it's the same business except that it gives preference to the company that can borrow the money at a lower rate than the client could. They are selling their own low fixed lending rate and buying the variable rate on the equity side.

At any point, anywhere in this process, the winners and losers are easy to identify in the abstract. The winners are those who make their decisions at those moment when they have more information about what stock prices should be than their competition, and the losers are the irrational actors, and those acting with poor quality information.

This idea, that profit is derived from exploiting the inefficient decision making of others, has an important impact on how the hedge fund industry thinks about which strategies have a long-term viability and which (probably) don't. Hedge funds exploit an information advantage. Market areas that are less efficient than they could be is where that information advantage is applied. Through some methodology, successful hedge fund trading strategies translate information into a better reflection of the fair price, and react to any difference there may be between that and the current market price.

The efficiencies listed in this example are clearly more sophisticated than anything currently happening in the Ad market. There is a wealth of other strategies being employed by institutions that are all designed to aggregate information in a way that provides an explicit information advantage, and to convert that advantage into a market generated (risky and variable) profit that benefits their investors. Abstractly speaking, when those strategies take a profit, it's the degree of added efficiency that they're being paid for.

It's precisely the same with hedge funds. The most profitable, most durable, and longest lasting strategies are those that provide the greatest information advantage in a way that makes use of that advantage in a captive manner much like those specializing in our fictional ad market. If you're tapping information that no one (or at least very few people) have access to, that's going to be viewed as a more promising strategy by industry allocators.

The degree of increased efficiency is reflective of the amount of money which can be made on the strategy, and the degree and manner used to obtain the information advantage can provide a key perspective on the length of time the strategy will probably operate before it's efficiency will begin to be crowded out by competition.

Which isn't to say that the act of finding new efficiencies can go on indefinitely. There is a lower limit to this thinking. To use the previous example of the Ad market, there will come a point where an advertiser will no longer be willing to pay for an additional optimization that gives them a tiny increase in sales because the cost of switching to that system will be higher than the extra return generated by the change.

In the capital markets this final remaining margin is

sometimes described as, market friction. This is the point at which the minimum fixed cost to engage in the business, no longer justifies the cost of getting into the business itself. And when the market is fully optimized given all the data available, that market is said to have reached the practical limits of peak pricing efficiency in that specific domain. But that doesn't mean that opportunity doesn't still exist in others.

People behaving in groups are remarkably predictable. Advertising success is a Pareto distribution, so in theory (though maybe not in practice due to other market effects) there is someone out there at any moment for whom a specific Ad will achieve a 100% success rate. If you can identify enough of those specific users there's always room in the marketplace. And so long as this is true, (and it's still very much true in every market I've ever heard of) there can still be an opportunity for greater efficiency. All you really have to do, is be better at identifying that person and that relevant moment in a supremely optimal way.

Suppose you could do just that. Suppose you had a means of teasing out the perfect moment when an Ad shown to a social media user will be 100% effective. Now you have a slightly different question to answer than the people who, in the past, had been looking for added efficiency. The question you want to answer now is, can you identify enough of the combination of users and moments, to engage in enough trading to justify an entire business?

This is, with some specifics aside, more or less the philosophical point where quantitative hedge funds are now in most liquid financial markets.

But this isn't a static or permanent circumstance. All it means is that the industry has reached a point where the current thinking requires some breakthrough to find a new way to approach the question. Thinking about it in exactly the same way everyone else does isn't going to bring you a great windfall like it might when those market inefficiencies were still untapped. But those incentives and the inefficiencies they create, all evolve and change over time. So that breakthrough is out there. It's always out there. Let's talk about some likely ways to find it.

Efficiency and Strategy Design

There are some rules of thumb for thinking about the design of quant strategies, though none are set in stone. Broadly speaking, a smaller market will have less native market efficiency, and the opportunities available will be somewhat larger on a percentage basis for someone who finds a way to add a new one, but the market's smaller size may limit the total dollars that can be extracted for each new efficiency added. A larger market, may have smaller opportunities on a percentage basis, and much more native efficiency, but the dollars extracted may turn out to be greater. The comparison to generating a 10% gain in a 10-Billion-dollar market or a 1% gain in a 100-Billion-dollar market is a good analogy.

But another consideration for a working strategy is the question of how long it will be profitable. A more liquid and efficient market will generally have higher participation overall which means a greater number of people all seeking out that new 1% gain. That means a new efficiency once identified, will usually have a shorter time period before others also discover it, and its performance begins to degrade for each person exploiting the newly discovered inefficiency.

10,000 people working at once to identify the same predictive signal are much more likely to find it, and find it quickly, than if only 10 people are looking for it. If that signal is a result of some new data becoming available or a new methodology identified for exploiting it, so many people are working in institutional finance that they will often find a signal close to simultaneously.

Since this is so, there is an argument for basing your strategy on some information which requires a unique advantage to acquire. Either some data which is difficult to come by, restricting the number of people who can access it, or some new technology which fewer people other than you, are able to make use of. Any exclusivity works to your advantage. Your goal should be to derive private knowledge about the structure of the market's current incentives and to do your best to keep it to yourself. Some piece of useful information that can be available to you alone. To the degree you can possess that private expertise, profit will be more likely and more sustained.

Which is to say that peak pricing efficiency isn't a static thing. Markets change, and with them, incentives change as well. As those conditions change and the incentives change with them, it creates opportunities where none existed before. Someone looking to find a new efficiency just needs to think a little further outside the box than others have in the past.

High Frequency Trading is one first-rate example. It came about as a result of breakthroughs in communications. Statistical Arbitrage was a product of the increasing computer power, and can be thought of as a function of Moore's law. Every time a breakthrough is found in some scientific area, if it can be applied at some level to trading, then it's likely to change the shape of the incentives and efficiencies available to others.

At the moment, the industry is still going through one such revolution and a wealth of opportunities are being created by it. Over the last 10 years or so, the hedge fund industry has come to understand that there is a wide array of new data available to traders from outside the domain of relative market pricing, and that data is allowing some to get way out in front of their competition and to create a substantial information advantage.

The rise of the data economy has meant dramatic changes for hedge funds. In the distant past, most trading analytics were a product of patterns derived from price and volume data because they were the only window into investor cognition that was available. Technical analysis is a legacy of that effort, and predates computers by decades. When there was nowhere else to look for insight, traders had to derive whatever correlation to investor cognition they could, and they did it from the patterns present in their trading history.

The modern criticism of technical analysis is that these patterns may tell you something, but what exactly? It may offer a window into the disposition of investors who are still wedded to it as a form of analysis, but little else. And as a greater and greater portion of transaction volume is controlled by rational institutions making rational choices independent of those signals, their effectiveness as an indicator has continued to decline. The arrival of computers in the finance industry and with it probabilistic quantitative finance, was probably the final nail in that coffin. And at the same time, it opened the industry's eyes to the wealth of other data which was rapidly becoming available.

When I joined Moore capital in the late 90's, the research team I led, included several staffers whose entire job was to spend

8 hours a day, every day, transcribing information that could only be obtained in printed format, into the vast research systems that the firm used for analysis. The firm knew the data had value, but in those early days when the internet was still young, there was no way to automate the input, so a meaningful portion of it was done manually.

That represented a substantial investment on the firm's part. But like every other investment, the firm viewed it as a swap. Pay up front for the subscriptions, the systems, and the staff, and get a return delivered in the form of an information advantage over competition, thanks to rapid delivery of sometimes complicated and detailed research. Studies that would take days or even weeks at other hedge funds could be produced at Moore Capital, usually in less than a few minutes.

The trading decisions that Moore Capital made were all supported by data. Moore was unique at the time in that it did no purely quantitative trading, but nearly every question that a discretionary PM had was followed up with a study designed to support or contradict it. If opinion X is true then the data should indicate Y. We performed Ad-hoc studies like this hundreds of times per week. Moore Capital was a data driven machine which used the expertise of its managers as the engine, and the data for evidence.

Since then, the focus on data driven decision making has spread from the hedge fund industry and has become prolific across all areas of the economy. You can often tell the leaders in a particular industry by who is most focused on data driven decision making. Jeff Bezos, a former DE Shaw quant, has made an entire career of treating Amazon like a quantitative hedge fund where data drives every decision. And in the process, he's made himself one of the wealthiest men in America.

Making the case for data driven decision making is no longer a challenge and when coupled with thoughtful predictive modeling, the options are endless. Social media, cellphone tracking, news reading and a vast variety of other datasets are all widely available to hedge funds, often at a very modest up-front price. Among the largest hedge funds, use of these non-financial datasets has become common. But these days the problem is less how to get the data, and more a question of figuring out how to derive useful information from it. Toward this end, some useful lessons can be taken from the few successful alt-data examples that have become publicly known.

One of the best-known success in the Alt-Data domain comes from a hedge fund strategy which specializes in the retail sector. They managed to get geo-located position statistics from cell phones, from which they derived foot traffic in and around the retailer's largest brick and mortar locations. People don't hang around retail stores for fun, so more people, they theorized, would probably mean more sales. Over time they were able to refine a predictive sales forecast for those companies, that was both considerably faster, and in many cases of higher quality, than the stores were able to produce for themselves through traditional internal means. They then used their expertise in the business models of the companies to trade these brick and mortar retailers in advance of their sales announcements.

In another well-known example, Commodity traders long ago began making limited use of satellite imagery to derive better forecast of supply – demand statistics for various crops. These days the larger funds are using AI for enhanced satellite imaging and weather analysis. The current models have become quite sophisticated, and have vastly outpaced the traditional methods used by the various government agencies charged with monitoring and reporting crop statistics.

NLP models for the analysis of live news feeds and social media posts have been around for a while as well, and they've become so prolific that it's hard to find a financial institution over a certain size which doesn't perform that kind of analysis at some level. Sentiment is usually the first stop for a team getting into this space, but it has a long-established track record of failing to predict markets. And as the percentage of volume managed by institutions has grown as compared to sentiment driven individuals directing their own trading, it's record has only gotten worse.

Which isn't to say that there isn't useful information content in both live news and social media, you'll just need to take a slightly more sophisticated view of human psychology to find it. It's people's behavior that reveals their true disposition, not what they say (particularly on social media). So, while you might not be able to tell what people's true opinions are from a post which complains or brags about their new iPhone, you can certainly tell that they bought a new iPhone or that they didn't buy an android device.

Alt-Data takes the entire universe of economic decision making taking place outside of the financial markets, and makes it into a disaggregated part of a single enormous model. Find a way to aggregate which brand of orange juice people will be likely to buy from their social media content, and to the degree you can predict it, you've achieved an information advantage. If you can predict sales with a specific accuracy, and model those companies with enough accuracy, you'll be in a position to better predict the stock price.

In spite of all the attention and effort that Alt-data is receiving now, the financial industry is really only just getting started with it, and there are no doubt huge opportunities which still remain to be exploited.

Among the more promising sounding ideas I've heard in the Alt-data domain involve things like analyzing over the road trucking statistics via tolls paid, or even the varying rates per mile for hiring a truck. Amazon itself has a substantial effort in this area, and is attempting to do what they've done in other areas to the increasingly liquid shipping brokerage industry. Though it hasn't been widely adopted yet, there is even an effort to list a shipping mile future on futures exchanges. Shipping port statistics can likewise probably be mined. If Amazon is doing it, and they are, then it's highly likely to be a fruitful area or research to some degree.

By far the biggest problem with Alt-data is that there is so much of it. In first world countries, tech advances are being used to document and collate the entirety of the human experience as cogs in an economic machine. While investors are only a small subset of people (and institutional investors are an even smaller set) there is bound to be a wealth of data that can be thoughtfully applied to economic activity. Far too much to list here. The key is to use it to attempt to derive actual human activity, which is a much more useful piece of knowledge than any sentiment.

In aggregate, investors are rational and institutional investors almost exclusively so. If you can find a way to use alternative data sources to expose knowledge that the predictors are using to derive their predictions, it might be possible for you to forecast their rational reactions to changes in it.

There's nothing I'd love better than to say to you "try this data or that data". But that simply isn't possible. What I can say though is that whatever your first instinct is, it should probably be thrown out. Even if you don't want to give your competition any credit for brains at all, you have to imagine they've tried the easy stuff.

Sentiment will tell you close to nothing. Who cares what some low information high school kid in Idaho thinks MSFT is going to do? The velocity of news might be more fruitful. Important ideas spread rapidly, and the more rapid, maybe the more important. Maybe predicting the bad decisions of irrational actors is enough and you can be on the other side from them.

One way or the other though, you should focus on gaining an information advantage that others are likely to miss. Remember, the people doing the analysis are all making the same mistakes at some point, in the logical chain of thought. There's no point in scurrying along behind them doing the same things they are, only more slowly.

In the financial markets the people whose behavior you most want to predict won't tell you in advance what they're thinking. And if they are willing to tell you they're probably just talking up their book, and you might not really want to know it. But if you can find a way to figure out what they're looking at when they think about it in the first place, there might be data relationship you can expose.

Maybe think about tagging people's identities in ways that are counterintuitive. Find a means of ranking them that gives you either a normal or Pareto distribution in some counter intuitive way. That, I believe, will inevitably be a source of tremendous profit.

Beyond that there's really only one useful piece of advice I can give you with regard to Alt-Data. The more you rely on other companies that sell data to provide you a specific dimension or pre-calculated analytic, the more that analytic will also be available to others and be of little likely value to you. Buy a fully tagged dataset from a company in that business, and anyone who ponies up the fee will have it too. That will make you one person among many, with no advantage whatsoever over the people you're competing with. And it's hard to outsmart everyone when you're all looking at the same thing, at the same time, in the same way.

When you decide to make a trade, there are is a broad spectrum of other investors with other incentives whose market participation will have an effect on the price you pay. Instead of rambling on about how their own interests look to each of them, I thought it might be more concise to walk through a fictitious trade example, complete with descriptions of how their interest would look to you from your perspective, if you were temporarily omniscient. Though this is a fictional example, every circumstance you'll read is taken from events I've witnessed personally in the live trading market.

The goal is to give you a window into how strategies which are dissimilar to yours provide a foothold for you in gaining an advantage. No strategy is perfect. They all have weaknesses. And your goal should be developing a strategy which makes use of these weaknesses where possible.

On Tuesday, at 9:29:59[2] eastern time, the multibillion dollar (fictitious) food conglomerate Daniel Archery-Northland (DANF) announces its earnings, ahead of their 10:00AM EST scheduled conference call. The headline published on all the news

---

[2] Companies don't announce earnings at market open. The time was chosen in order to provide as much clarity as possible and to prevent any assumptions about other external information changes. It's the one event in the timeline which is truly fictional.

services says that they've beat expectations by 31c per share – a sizable earnings beat.

Your automated trading system has been tracking companies that beat earnings, and since your technical analysis shows DANF on an upward trajectory, the news of the earnings beat causes your system to authorize a buy. You run a day trading system. So, in every buy there is an implicit sell which will be scheduled for something close to the end of the day.

Since your system is fully automated, the order is automatically created and submitted to your broker to be filled at the open, without human intervention. The process takes a total of 500 milliseconds from the first moment you see the headline, but since the decision to buy was made, your lightning fast systems took only 5 milliseconds to generate and send the order.

Your broker's order management system instantly forwards the order along to the exchanges, where it's entered in the order book behind a few other limit orders at that price, which were already present when yours arrived. The current bid-offer on DANF is 49.40 – 49.41, and your order is for 5,000 shares at 49.405. That's a larger order than the market for DANF can normally accommodate at once, but earnings announcements always increase volume, so you feel good about getting the order fully filled.

The exchange market maker's systems receive your order, and enters it in the order book at the price you've set. Before the order can be acted upon by the exchange systems, the market maker sends a confirmation receipt to your broker's EMS, indicating that the communication was successful and the order has been received. The market maker is a high frequency liquidity provisioner that runs ultra-high-speed systems in all the geographically dispersed exchanges.

Total time lapsed: 6 milliseconds. DANF Bid – Offer: 49.40 – 49.41

If the market maker were to take the event of your order's arrival in the market and use that to drive its own orders on other exchanges it would be illegal, so it doesn't. Instead, it uses its own system's internal event of a generation of a confirmation receipt, to drive all further action within its system. That difference costs them a total of 410 microseconds on every transaction, but it technically eliminates any accusation of front running, lowering the regulatory risk. When they were designing the system they literally imagined an SEC investigator saying "Do you use the arrival of that order to drive any logic in your system pertaining to other orders?" If they're ever asked that question, they will confidently reply "No".

They HF market maker has been monitoring the news as well, and since being faster is the singular goal of their systems, their systems are an order of magnitude faster than yours. So, while the analysis of the headline was still being processed by the much slower systems in the various hedge funds (including yours), their system was scanning the prices for DANF in all the less frequently used exchanges and dark pools. In anticipation of an increase in buy volume generated by the news, they placed their own buy orders at the lower effective range of the bid offer spread, wherever those other exchange prices were below the prices at the primary exchange.

Technically, there is no front running occurring. All that's happening is they're reacting to the news faster than you are, and being more specific about where their orders are placed. And since their orders are arriving at those remote exchanges first, they're buying up any of the lower priced shares that are available. By the time the orders on the NYSE are ready to be acted upon, they've already accumulated a low-priced inventory of shares to meet the increase in demand that's only milliseconds away.

They bought their stock in places like Kansas City and Philadelphia, as well as the half dozen dark pools that are run by the money center banks, all of which they have access to. On average, they paid 49.403 per share. So, when their system sells those same shares to you from their inventory at the NYSE a few milliseconds later, they can do so at 49.4144 - below the limit price specified on your order, and still make a tiny profit per share.

Since they specified prices with their orders, all their orders were filled as limit orders, so in addition to a small profit, they will also inevitably collect an additional .6 cent per share rebate from the exchange as well. And thanks to their ability to predict the flow of future orders (their solitary business expertise), after filling your order, they still have a sizable position in DANF left to accommodate all the people who are your direct competition, but run slightly slower systems, and haven't reacted to the new information as rapidly as you.

Total time lapsed: 13 milliseconds. DANF Bid – Offer: 49.4 – 50.01
Your DANF Profit: $0.00

Your order is filled by the exchange. You got all the shares you wanted at the price you specified. A filled receipt is received by you 3 seconds later, and according to your market data provider, the stock price has begun to move. Many people had been looking for the DANF announcement but thanks to your tech expertise, you were faster, so you already had your shares bought at your price when they finally arrived to do the same. As those orders are filled by the liquidity provisioner, you watch the price begin to move higher.

Total time lapsed: 3 seconds. DANF Bid – Offer: 49.53 – 50.34
Your DANF Profit: $650.00

From second to second you see the bid offer prices gap up.

The offer price has risen nearly 70 cents, while the bid price has risen just 13 cents. Most of the new orders are buy orders so the last price is shown as the offer of 50.34, but you know you can only get filled on a sell at the bid. That means that your total capital at risk is $247,050, and you're currently at a profit of $650, or 0.263% on the trade. Not the superstar home run you were hoping for yet, but not bad for a few seconds work.

Since a bird in the hand is worth two in the bush, you decide to submit an order to try to sell your shares at the slightly higher price. Maybe you can get lucky on the bid offer spread. Your order arrives at the exchange to sell, but by this time, traditional market makers who are slower than the HF market maker, have had time to react to the news as well. They have no interest in simply giving money to their high frequency competitors by offering pricing which is away from the market, so the bid offer spread gaps further.

Since you just submitted a sell order, the market makers see its arrival behind a few others of the same price, and react to it by dropping the bid. Before your order can be executed, bid price falls again to 49.38, just below your cost. You're swimming in the market maker's pond now and they have great expertise in managing the bid-offer.

Their system is based exclusively on deriving the velocity of the orders arriving in the order book. Your system doesn't even look at this data, so they have a momentary advantage over you and your sell order doesn't fill. There are still buy orders arriving from the slower buyers who are still reacting to the news, so the offer price remains high as the market makers try to accumulate their own shares at the other end of the bid-offer spread, in order to sell to them.

Since the bid offer gap has increased so much, your limit order is never executed. After a minute or so, you submit a cancel and go with your original plan of holding to the end of the day. But the instant you cancel your sell order it changes the dimensions of the order book and the HF market maker reacts to that change, causing the bid price flicker above your limit for the (now deleted) sell order but only for an instant, so it seems to you like it might have been a mirage. In reality is was the HF system picking off a higher sell order in a dark pool, but just for 100 shares. The slower primary exchange market makers are defining the spread, and it stays below your price level for any new sellers.

**Total time lapsed: 2 minutes: DANF Bid – Offer: 49.38 – 50.34
Your DANF Profit: -$100.00**

Buried in the story of the DANF earnings announcement but not featured in the headline, was another piece of information. Cloaked in vague sounding language was a comment by the CEO that their continued expenses in their new GMO Soybean initiative are being treated as part of a long-term strategy for the company, and "should not have much impact on their forward guidance for the rest of the year, in spite of declining trade relationship with China" – their principle buyer.

Those systems that read the news for sentiment are slower than yours, and read this as a positive statement. "No impact on forward guidance." It's still only three minutes since the announcement.

But more detailed analysis requires more time. So now, even slower and more accurate NLP systems are comparing this comment to previous comments from the CEO on the same initiative, and to those systems, this seems a much more guarded comment. Since they know their analysis will take longer, even if it's just a few seconds, these slower systems are run by investors who maintain a longer average holding period per trade than the fast systems, and they try to create their information advantage by being more accurate.

The slow NLP systems believe this comment raises the risk of a decline in forward guidance and since prices have just seen a spike, they decide to trade the downside risk rather than the buy side. They place some limit orders to sell near the peak offer price, in anticipation discretionary traders who they know from long experience, are doing the same thing they are and will come to the same conclusions that they have, albeit more slowly. The discretionary traders will have to read the actual article themselves after all, and that takes longer than reading it by machine.

Now instead of the order book showing a much larger aggregate investor interest on the bid side - pushing prices higher, the order book has returned to a net neutral weighting with both bid and offer showing the increase in volume that everyone expected following the news.

However, the bid side and the offer side haven't changed in the same way or at the same rate. The bid order volume (increase in buyers) over the last few milliseconds, rose gently to a peak and then began to decline, mimicking the right side of a normal distribution with the rate of change now in decline. While the offer side (more sellers than buyers) spiked suddenly nearly a minute afterward, indicating that more volume is yet due to follow it. One person reacts first, a few more next, and so on. So, the two normal distributions of investor reaction time are offset from one another. Over extremely short-term time horizons, buying looks to be drying up, but selling still seems to be on the upswing.

The high frequency systems react to that in just another 10 milliseconds doing the opposite of what they did when the story broke, and generating more profit on the downside in Philadelphia, Chicago, Kansas City, and in the dark pools. They have sold off their accumulated inventory during the price spike, and apart from netting out the simultaneous trades available across the exchanges, are now selling the stock short at the higher price, in anticipation of buying it back when the selling volume reaches its peak.

The various other market maker systems may be slow compared to those doing liquidity provisioning, but it's been a full three minutes since the announcement so they've had time to react as well. Now all the market makers have begun to pressure the NYSE price on the downside with the HF systems leading the way. Last executed price: 49.35.

Total time lapsed: 3 minutes: DANF Bid – Offer: 49.21 – 49.35
Your DANF Profit: -$250.00

Unlike the liquidity provisioning systems, the market making systems aren't trying to perform riskless arbitrage on two separate exchanges at the same time. They're generating a forward-looking projection on price movement from order book velocity. This forecast is for a relatively short period of time, at most just a few seconds. But that forward-looking probability is less certain than the riskless execution the liquidity provisioners strive for.

The high frequency players aren't just faster than you, they're faster than the other market makers as well. Faster is their only game. So, while traditional market makers are continuing to push the price even lower, the liquidity provisioners have switched sides again and are using their speed advantage to keep the various exchanges in sync. The net effect of this is to apply a mean reversion pressure to prices. If the price drops suddenly they tend to buy the low, and if it spikes suddenly they sell the high. As we pass the three-minute mark, price volatility per millisecond has begun to decline and the HF orders have begun to moderate the selling of the traditional market makers. This has the effect of stabilizing the price for a minute or so. Last Price: 49.31

Total time lapsed: 3.1 minutes: DANF Bid – Offer: 49.31 – 49.43
Your DANF Profit: -$450.00

It's only been 3.1 minutes since the news has been announced. Compared to program trading systems, discretionary traders are even slower to react, but their business models compensate for this with comparatively long hold times and superior precision of their forecasts.

By now, the fastest of them have read the whole news story, decided what they thought the CEO's ambiguous comments probably meant, and have decided to hedge their exposure a bit in anticipation of the earnings call, which is still 26.5 minutes away.

Some discretionary hedge fund traders who already hold the stock have been following the announcement closely. They've begun buying puts on DANF in case the substance of the call inspires them to sell out. This causes the price of puts to rise slightly, but each of the option market makers has an interest in the underlying as well. They have no desire to get caught out at a loss, so they hedge their positions with the cash equity. They buy shares in the market in order to hedge a portion of their short put options exposure, but the hedge funds who are buying puts and selling shares and the hedge funds represent a much larger risk pool than option market makers. So more selling volume is arriving in the market and the market makers are covering only a portion of it. Overall DANF volume is dropping from its post news peak when the HF systems were cranked up to 11 and executing orders at multiple exchanges for the same price just to receive the rebate. And as the rate of change in the order book slows, the bid offer spread on DANF begins to tighten again. Last Price: 49.31

Total time lapsed: 9 minutes: DANF Bid – Offer: 49.28 – 49.32
Your DANF Profit: -$600.00

The S&P Index hasn't changed much in the last 9 minutes, but DANF has. So much in fact, that the systems of the managers of the two most popular S&P index ETF's have noticed the gap. They can now buy the constituents of both the broad index ETF and the agro ETF's (of which DANF is a large part) and sell the ETF in the market for a riskless arbitrage. Their participation in the markets begins to push the indexes down slightly, linking a beta affect to the drop of DANF. That buying pressure stabilizes the market for DANF, compressing the bid offer spread. And since the market overall has begun to dip slightly, to some other investors who track the beta relationship carefully, it seems to be exerting an influence on DANF pricing. All of these investors act on their knowledge in varying amounts. And although the spread is tightening, both bid and offer fall slightly in response to the change in the SPY.

Total time lapsed: 19 minutes: DANF Bid – Offer: 49.11 – 49.14
Your DANF Profit: -$1,450.00

As the clock ticks on in anticipation of the call, there is no new information with regard to DANF. The price begins to oscillate, but not much. It stays mostly within the bid offer spread as various tiny market participants react to the news, the sentiment created by it, or other information. No one is taking any big chances ahead of the earnings call, with so little new information currently arriving.

Various players with various speed advantages over others try to nudge the market this way and that, trying to lure new investors into the market. The HF market makers make a new decision every 10 milliseconds, the traditional market makers every 500 milliseconds, and the arbitrageurs every second or so on average. But without much new money or new information external to the market and with the anticipated rush of information that may come from the call, prices tend to bounce back and forth between the bid and offer without a firm trend one way or the other. Everything seems to be on hold in anticipation of the earnings call, and the new information it might bring.

The investors with the largest stake in DANF are large long-term value investors. They have hedged their broader market position so they aren't worried about the tiny oscillations. Huge fund manager GreyRock Inc, and the famous Belgian investor Wilhelm Banquette (sometimes referred to as the Augur of Antwerp) and several other very big players, all have stakes in the massive company as part of their long-term interest in controlling the world's food supply. But things in global trade aren't what they used to be, and they need to take opportunities where they find them.

Banquette isn't much for options speculation. Derivatives are morally wrong as far as he's concerned, and he says so out loud on every one of those rare occasions that he meets a journalist who he believes is sober enough to remember it. But morals notwithstanding, selling a few covered calls on their position is a nice low risk trade.

The firm has a policy against option speculation as a strategy, but the execution trader who works for Banquette knows better. He knows he gets paid on P&L, not domination of the global food supply, and his only explicit limitation is based on his cumulative risk. He has wide latitude to affect trading so long as total risks stay below a defined metric.

He's also overheard some grumblings from the agro

analysis team and he knows the big guy isn't quite as keen on the sector as he used to be. The boss can be impetuous, emotional and volatile, so he doesn't want to end up on the wrong side of him unprepared if things go wrong. He isn't allowed to decide what to put a major investment in, but managing the execution of that investment and assuring low impact to pricing when it happens, is exactly what he's there for.

The sudden move in price for DANF options has caused a gap between put prices and call prices, so he seizes the opportunity and sells some calls for a small portion of the firm's overall position. Since the firm has such a big position in the cash equity, it's technically a risk reduction move so he's covered on the letter of his instructions and well within his dollar limitations for risk. If things on his options trade go against him, he's confident he can get out of a small trade like his that quickly, with a minimum of loss.

He runs a quick liquidity study for DANF using the firms' massive new risk management system and that tells him how much in dollars he can expect to sell if he were selling throughout the day with a minimum of market impact. He knows it's wrong, but it gives him an idea of what to expect. Then, just one minute before the earnings conference call, he becomes a covered call option seller and hedges his small trade.

Small is a relative term. A small trade to Banquette's massive multibillion-dollar firm isn't the kind of trade that would look small to everyone. But Banquette's trader knows he'll have all day to net it out if it goes badly, so he's constrained by a different level of volume that the market makers or high-speed traders who are worried about what the order book is doing over just the next few milliseconds.

He pulls the trigger, and sells calls against 45 million of the firm's 1.9-billion-dollar position, confident that no one who matters in the marketplace will notice such a small amount. The options order traffic causes the option market makers to act again, hedging that side of their risk. And that puts even more downward pressure on DANF prices, and compresses the bid offer spread a bit further.

Total time lapsed: 29 minutes: DANF Bid – Offer: 49.08 – 49.11
Your DANF Profit: -$1,600.00

Meanwhile, you've been staring at your screen mystified. "They beat earnings and the price drops nearly $0.40 per share! What the hell is wrong with these people ... they must be insane!! It's right there in the headline, earnings beat 32 cents per share ... that's 2.4 billion dollars! WTF!!! Don't these people like making money?"

You've been following the technical indicators closely and you know that a sudden move in any direction is often followed by a mean reversion. Since the stock has been down, you've been hoping to see that reversion begin. The RSI and the MACD both indicate that it's close.

In the stress of the moment with a losing trade on the books, it hasn't occurred to you that mean reversion only happens when all other things are equal, and in this case, there is new news which indicated that there might be some forward-looking downside risk that hasn't been valued into the price. So instead of selling out at a loss right now, you bite the bullet, watch your DMA channel and other technical indicators closely, and sit tight hoping for someone, somewhere, to return to their senses and buy this stock like they would in a sane world.

10:00 AM Earnings call:

Comments by the DANF CEO breeze over the forward-looking guidance, where he claims that the company has carefully budgeted the new expenditures as a 5-year plan, and the accounting may show some negative numbers in the detail for upcoming quarters, but they expect that to be fully offset by other positives that they plan to see during those periods. They get through the prepared remarks on the call and the Q&A begins. The first question is from a first-year analyst on the agro team from mid-sized equity broker, Andelman-Schwarz.

"Yes, you say the expenditures for the GMO Soybean

program will be offset by other positives. Assuming the state of trade relations in China don't change going forward, do you have any idea how long it will take to see the fully realized return on that program?"

The CEO's voice is calm and measured. In the background behind him, you thought you heard someone else's voice whispering "Who the F*** is this kid, get me his boss on the phone NOW!" but it was hushed by the voice of the CEO, and difficult to make out clearly.

The CEO then calmly and rationally explained that though they're unhappy with the current situation with regard to China trade, soybean supplies seem a reliable import for them and they believe it will be one of the last items effected by the declining relationship.

"Our expectation is that the revenue expected from the program will come to fruition no more than 1 year later than expected, but in an absolute worst case, it could be as much as three years, and our budgeting will be managed accordingly so it shouldn't affect the bottom line for investors or have any noticeable impact on earnings."

Total time lapsed: 92 minutes: DANF Bid – Offer: 49.16 – 49.19
Your DANF Profit: -$1,200.00

After being calmed somewhat by the CEO's comments,

most traders move on. Those that bought at the lows took their profits, those that didn't took to social media to tell all their friends that prices may have been pushed lower by "bedwetting cucks", but it's on an uptrend for the last 2 minutes, so things look bright. A few other investors inspired by the calming technical analysis, bought in as well, but volume has fallen off dramatically since the pre-earnings call surge. Bombastic TV analysts on CNBC are describing the call as a "nothing burger".

Meanwhile, from his massive lair constructed beneath Belgium's only active volcano, legendary straight-shooting value investor Wilhelm Banquette sits stroking his hairless cat, and has been having other thoughts. He has spoken to the CEO many times and he thought he heard a little something in his tone. The emotional reaction he heard in the background of the call gave him further pause. He couldn't make it out precisely, but then, he didn't have to.

As it stands, he's decided between cat strokes, that he's not at all convinced that the CEO's analysis is as straightforward as it seems. And besides, he's never liked that guy. The vague language of "NOTICABLE impact on earnings" rubbed him the wrong way. "Being an oligarch has its advantages", he thinks to himself. And, he then instructs his people to give the CEO a bit of a wrist slap, and puts in an order to sell 20% of their total position, 375 million dollars worth of shares at current pricing.

When he gets the order from the boss, his execution trader

pats himself on the back for anticipating his view and locking in some profit ahead with his option selling. He puts in an order to sell the remaining position on a day long VWAP algorithm with their broker's execution system. For each of the 300 or so minutes of the trading day, commensurate with the average volume per minute, they'll be adding roughly 1.1 Million dollars of selling pressure.

Volume has dropped precariously since the mad rush at the open, but his execution algo is well designed. Every time the various shorter-term players try to push the price up, another million in shares arrives to make the most of the rising price pressure and minimize the downward impact of the sell. The profit locked in by his early call selling has effectively ensured net neutral market impact for him on the day.

Bit by bit as news of the large seller gets out, all the market makers correctly see the writing on the wall and they drop the price a bit more, and a bit more, but only in small increments so as not to increase their exposure.

Gone is the excess volatility that was coupled with the big news from the earnings call, so to people like you watching the price on their terminals, rather than seeming like the price is going over a waterfall, the price instead seems to be grinding slowly downward, more and more, for all but the last few minutes of the day. The market makers are managing their inventory with an eye toward netting it all out when the leveraged day traders have to close their positions near the close.

Total time lapsed: 388 minutes: DANF Bid – Offer: 47.48 – 47.51
Your DANF Profit: -$9,600.00

The close is fast approaching. Two minutes left. You've been hoping to see a spike in the price but so far it hasn't come. Every time the price would rise 5 cents or so, it would fall 7 cents in the next few seconds, and it's been impossible to get ahead of it.

Volume has been disastrously small, far too small for you to execute your 5,000-share position without signaling to the whole world that there is a seller, giving them all knowledge they need to move the bid offer lower in reaction to it and keeping you from being executed. You expect that would cause the high frequency players to crush the price lower. Average volume is just 1,000 shares a minute. Then comes the last two minutes.

Volume spikes at the close the same as always, but for some reason the price doesn't do the same. Over the course of the day, every market maker, day trader, broker, hedge fund manager, and value investor has been hearing a rumor of a large seller in the market for DANF. Some people have speculated that it might be Willhelm Banquette, sending a signal to the DANF CEO. Everyone knows Banquette's always hated that guy.

More to the point, the market makers know there are a bunch of people out there who bought at a much higher price than the current market. They know this because that was the moment they shorted the stock to sell it to them. They know that all they have to do is keep the price from meaningfully rising and the least informed investors, many of whom bought on the news using leverage, will have to sell out to them locking in the profits on their short positions. Unless new buyers enter the marketplace, they'll be fine, and with all that news in the rearview mirror, finding a new buyer of any meaningful size is unlikely. On top of all this, Banquette's algo hasn't been able to execute all it's selling so it's trying to make up the difference.

Suddenly you're faced with a decision. Do you book the substantial loss or do you hold the position overnight? The technical charts aren't much help to you. There is no new news. Sentiment on social media since the call has all been positive and lots of people are talking about the technical trend, but for some reason you can't fathom, it hasn't affected the stock price. Someone must be "manipulating" the market to screw you.

You're faced with the hard choice of taking a punishing loss right now, or face the potential of an even more catastrophic loss tomorrow. You hope things will improve, but you know that hope isn't a business plan. So instead, you grit your teeth, take a deep breath and accept the roughly 10K loss.

This is a fictitious scenario, but all the specifics come from actual trading and real-life circumstances. I didn't invent any of those events, decision making chains or timelines. Every one of them was personally witnessed by me at some point, and I only pulled them together into a single day for illustration. If there was any point in this description where you said to yourself "No way, that would never happen!" I can assure you, you're absolutely mistaken. Every single one of those things did happen. I saw them all with my own eyes.

In bringing this timeline of events together into a single day and single stock while giving you full visibility to the decisions of others instead of the "none" you get in real life, I've tried to highlight some of the important misconceptions about how the incentives for investors vary with regard to a single new piece of information. First and foremost, among those differences having an impact on incentives, is their anticipated holding period of a trade.

High frequency traders are at the most extreme end of this distribution. If they make a new trade decision once every 5 milliseconds, they can make as many as 4,680,000 decisions per day, per stock. They won't make much per trade, but at that frequency of trading, they don't have to. As market makers, they are exchange members so there is no commission directly to them to speak of.

In the example above, assuming no other trade volume than what's shown, they will make 65 dollars on that trade. In real life, there will be lots of other volume, information and interest to moderate that. But multiply that by nearly 5 million decisions a day and it starts to add up. Of course, they won't win on every trade. No one wins all the time not even high frequency traders. But at even a fairly modest hit rate their profit adds up quickly.

On the other end of the spectrum, slower traders may not make trades as often, but their low trade rate gives them copious time to get to know every relevant detail that pertains to a company. Even subtle and non-quantifiable issues like a tone of voice with regard to an earnings call might be enough for them to form some relevant opinion and to act on it. When they do, they can do so at spectacular size relative to other shorter-term traders. So, although they may look relatively inefficient in the short term, thanks to their comparatively massive position sizes, their profitability on the long term can be spectacular, and the results can often drive headlines in the business press.

For them the bigger issue is managing the volatility that comes with holding large positions over a long holding period. And the problem with hedges is that they turn out to be very expensive relative to the protection they offer. In a perfectly efficient market, the cost of a hedge is exactly equal to the downside protection if offers. But the market isn't perfectly efficient. And thanks to fat tailed distributions, hedges are only ever estimated and tend to break down the most when you need them the most. So, there is considerably effort expended on the quant side every year, trying to find optimum ways to hedge in the most cost-effective way, and still have the hedge be effective when things fall apart.

Meanwhile, although every player in the space has some direct competition, and they want to be faster than them in aggregate, the rest of the players in the market aren't really competition in that way at all. Each group of investors reacts to new news in a roughly normally distributed way, but the only people in that distribution are investors with a similar set of incentives to theirs. They don't really compete for reaction time at all with those market participants who have differing time dimensions to their decisions.

I hope the conclusion is obvious. Though the business models and incentives of each player in the market dynamic gives them real advantage in certain circumstance, it creates profound weaknesses for them in others. And it's often the gaps between one class of investors and another which provides opportunity for a new player or strategy to enter the space.

So how do you, a new player in the market, find a new way to exploit this? It's an industry axiom that being a good quant isn't about getting the answers right. Anyone can get the answers right, or hire someone to get them for him. The key to being a good quant is asking the right questions. And one potentially very useful question to ask yourself when looking to create a new information advantage is this: "What are they doing wrong?"

Every existing strategy has weaknesses and places where the assumptions of the strategy offer an opportunity to others.

One mistake in that narrative that I wanted to call particular attention to was belief that everyone else was reacting to the news irrationally. These were all institutional players, and none of them were behaving irrationally. What they were doing was behaving rationally against a completely different set of decision making constraints imposed by differing incentives. And their business models were optimized to capture a completely different aspect of market inefficiency. The only people anyone was ever trying to beat, were the other market participants doing things exactly the same way they were. But in the process, they were each profiting from some small advantage over players with other incentives, that their specific business model gave them.

In the case of the long-term investors, their positions are so large that they often distort pricing in the short term whether they like it or not. There is only ever so much stock you can buy in a given period without moving the price. Predict when long term players are buying or selling, trade ahead of them with a shorter holding period in a smaller amount, and you may become as profitable on a hit rate basis as the HF systems, but with much larger positions and more volatility consumed. This will mean a much larger profit per trade.

In the case of the HF traders, their systems are fast, but there is only so much math you can do in the microsecond timeline they have available for a new decision and only so much data changes at all in that tiny window. Develop a way to more accurately forecast the price trajectory via any means, and you can wait out the HF systems and take money from them. These are just two off the cuff ideas, developed without any real energy applied at all. But it's an example of the best way to think about the interaction of the differing players in any market. And if you can design a system in this way or describe the system you've already designed to investors in this way, it will likely inspire great confidence in institutional investors.

So, in what way are the existing players making an error? What are they doing wrong? Which unproven assumptions are they all making, in a way that might be improved? Is there a better way to identify and hedge extraneous risks more cheaply, providing an advantage for longer held positions? Is there a way to use the limited time available to the high frequency players to identify opportunities in the short term, without necessarily beating them at their own game by being the fastest? All these are great design questions to ask.

And an even more important question may be this one. If you can create an opportunity like this by being faster or better than others, How long will it last? How long will it be before others in the space see the same information you do, and mimic your system forcing you to split a portion of the profit with them? The most successful models over the long term, are those which rely on some difficult to bridge information gap that leaves you more or less alone with your information advantage. Simple models may be easy to create, but they're easy for your competition to create as well.

Arguably the single most successful program trading application in terms of total profit since inception has been statistical arbitrage. When it was originally created, the methodology of statistical risk reduction was a complex and processor intensive dynamic which combined skills in math, technology, and data management that weren't typically available among 'market experts' of the day. Today, those skills are much more common, and the individual profitability of a new player in that strategy has been thinned, as many more players entered the space and the pricing inefficiencies exposed by it have become much more efficient.

But a similar dynamic exists today as well. And it will be found by exploiting those areas where the information advantage gained is supported, either directly or indirectly, by the limitations of a business model of another player. AI may eventually be that kind of advantage. Alt-Data will certainly be a part of it. But how long it last will always be about the information advantage created between the first person that identifies it, and the legion of other geniuses who will be hot on their tail immediately afterward.

Even the rant above about how crazy and irrational everyone else must be was a real-life event. This is what really happens out there in the real world. And since it's possible for us to see exactly what others are doing in this narrative where it isn't in the real world, it should be pretty easy to see where the errors are occurring, and how no particular investor or group of investors has an iron clad correct perspective on how a particular stock will respond to a new piece of information over time.

All there ever is, is a consensus based on the distribution of investors who are currently engaged in a trading decision, and the various incentives to which they're responding. All of those incentives leave plenty of room for the ambitious new player like you.

Wall Street Ethics

Whether they're actually smarter or not, market participants including successful hedge funds, have far greater knowledge about how their markets work than the people charged with regulating them. The entire 400 Billion dollar Swaps market and all the associated derivative products representing trillions in notional value are all a product of that philosophy and the entire market was specifically created that way, in order to get around accounting rules. How do you imagine "off balance sheet transactions" got "off balance sheet" in the first place?

Financial regulation in the institutional world, is typically viewed in a manner designed to expose any potential exceptions to it. Regulatory "wiggle room" is the order of the day. To call this perspective on regulatory risk widespread, understates it.

And as a result of this broad philosophy, there are many normal practices in the finance industry which might be considered unethical to business people from other backgrounds, but are none the less perfectly legal as practiced in 99% of all cases. They may violate the spirit of the law, but in most cases, they don't actually violate the letter, and the letter of the law is where enforcement happens.

Earlier I mentioned that a hedge fund's interests with brokers aren't perfectly aligned. Since most banks are also floor brokers on the exchanges, and are market makers for specific stocks, many of these practices come down to them. But they are by no means alone in these practices, nor by any stretch the worst offenders. The futures markets have been notorious for years for making the petty malfeasance committed on the equity trading floors look trivial by comparison, to say nothing of the overseas markets. And even their regulatory ambivalence is dwarfed in both dollar and percentage terms, by the universally accepted "mark to model" accounting standards in the over the counter fixed income space.

Many new players in the institutional financial markets take great exception to this when they learn the details. Some may consider it cheating, but to institutions it's simply considered the rules of the road. Civil enforcement is often about justifying costs. So, to institutions, if the minimum cost of enforcement is high enough, they know the rules will be largely ignored. No one likes it of course, but they learn to live with a bit of it in every area, confident that if someone is stealing, at least they won't be stealing much, and any change to the current regs is as likely to make things worse as better.

One old joke in this regard is the much-overused Hollywood story of the banker who figured out how to steal a fraction of a cent from every bank transaction by rounding them down to the penny, and taking the fractional penny remainder.

No one individual loses enough to make the time and energy

in pursuing a civil penalty worth it. So, the banker gets away with it, collecting millions in total profits from the miniscule transactions. In truth, both bank accounting systems and the business models of High Frequency traders both exploit this phenomenon for gain as a perfectly public part of their business models. In the bank's case, it's barely a blip on their massive balance sheets but for HF traders, it's a meaningful percentage of their annual profit.

I mention these issues because they're so often used as rationalizations for poor performance by new managers. But everyone else in capital markets trading can post their gains in spite of these lapses, and you should be able to as well. Unless you're trying to compete directly with the participants listed here, they are not a reason for your failure and you shouldn't view them as such. If you are competing directly with them, then the reason for your failure is that they're better at it than you are. Hopefully an explanation of how they work will make that somewhat easier to swallow.

If there is a sub section of the financial industry that's by far the most criticized, it's got to be High Frequency Traders. The business they're in can be best conceived of as a technology arms race. Spend the most money on communications and technology, and you will be fastest. Of course, if you are the fastest today then you'll be forced to spend the most money tomorrow as well, in order to remain the fastest. High Frequency trader's expenses are a product of Moore's law and the necessity of remaining on the bleeding edge.

The perfect trade for a HF system is to have a single asset for sale on two separate exchanges separated by geography, at two slightly differing prices, at exactly the same time. This allows them to buy it in one location and sell it in another simultaneously, making a tiny profit, while never holding any stock. If they ended the process with stock in their book, that would represent a forward-looking risk. That's going to happen to them a portion of the time and their models are designed to cope with the subsequent probabilities of gain or loss when it does. But all things being equal, they prefer riskless transactions.

As mentioned in the timeline from the last chapter, depending on the exchange they're trading on, a portion of their profits also come in the form of commission rebates generated by being liquidity providers on one of the exchanges that pays such rewards. Typically, a limit price order will meet the requirement for a rebate on either the NYSE or various NASDAQ exchanges. The exchanges pay out billions in rebates every year, much of it to HF firms.

When it comes to the other exchanges, much of the transaction volume generated by High Frequency teams are executed in dark pools. These are separate private exchanges, usually run by the big banks, which have grown out of those institution's block trading desks. They make that volume available for execution, but not available for price discovery, hence the darkness. At any given moment, a substantial portion of the stock that's available to buy or sell is actually in these dark pools, so there are more total shares available to trade at any given moment than the volume reporting ever indicates, but no one knows precisely how much. It's the HF traders that most often bring these shares into the market. Since the banks often have their own HF teams, access to the dark pools aren't usually a truly competitive space.

The riskless ideal HF trading scenario is common enough, but in order to extract as much money as possible, the typical HF team needs to go further. They will often monitor trade volume and pricing in order to try to predict where prices are going to go in the very, very short term. To do this they use a wide variety of ultra-fast statistical analysis systems. Different teams use different methodologies involving depth of book analysis, dollar momentum, bid offer spread forecasting and many, many others.

It has been widely reported that upon occasion some HF teams will pay retail brokers a fixed fee for their trade flow. The recent news centered around the Robin Hood trading application is the latest example. This practice allows HF traders to get a look at what retail investors want to buy and sell, the prices they want to buy and sell it, and gives them a microsecond of additional opportunity to place orders in advance of those trades.

That practice is known as front running. Technically, front

running is against the rules, which of course means that some quasi legal version of it that's just on this side of the letter of the law, happens every single day. Tens of thousands of transactions across a wide variety of markets and exchanges meet this criterion. But don't blame the high frequency traders for creating it. Front running has always happened, and it predates the high frequency trading by decades. If I had to bet, it was probably invented the day immediately after they invented the concept of a stock, an order, and an exchange.

There's an old Wall Street joke that says that the only mandatory dress code for floor brokers at the NYSE was a ski-mask, so no one could see who they were when they were robbing the place. Front running is one of those open secrets, and by no means have the High Frequency traders invented it or are even its worst practitioners in history.

The only thing that the rise of the HF traders really did was democratize the practice. Rather than just a few clients being front run by a comparatively large amount in some cases and not at all in others, (as often still happens in the futures and currency markets), instead, virtually all clients are front run virtually all the time, but are giving up only the tiniest percentage of their potential profit. Something akin to the man in the joke taking a fraction of a cent at the bank.

I don't have evidence of this next claim and there are vast interests ensuring it stays that way, but it's a broad-based industry assumption that this is exactly what happens on the majority of the 40% of total equity trading volume that the HF traders represent. In reality, this kind of treatment of regulatory constraints happens at all levels of the financial services industry, and the cause can be traced to a separate systemic market inefficiency of a slightly different sort.

The SEC is a civil enforcement bureau, so in order to extract a penalty there must be a victim who is willing to make a case of the alleged malfeasance. And that means that to bring an SEC action against a High Frequency trader accused of front running, there must be a documented loss. No documented loss, no cause for action.

The documentation is usually easy enough to produce, but front runners are very careful to keep the amount of loss low enough in each instance so at no time is the cost in both legal expenses and time, worth it to bring an action against them. In the worst cases, it's usually settled between institutions with an angry phone call and a commission give back of some sort. This is how the industry self regulates, and is one of the many reasons to remain on good terms with your prime broker.

This phenomenon is sometimes referred to in the technical and economic literature as part of market friction. It's the efficiency gap between the cost of the business, and its enforcement. If the friction for an individual client is kept low enough, and the reward for the sum of all client's friction is high enough, a high frequency trader can more or less operate with complete impunity, front running every single order they see, and never be brought to action for it.

From the side of those paying the friction, a nominal cost is worked into their business model in the same way that the industry deals with slippage. If you're buying a million shares of Amazon, holding it for a year, and expect to make 15 million dollars on it, why in the world will you care that you got a questionable execution that may have cost you $100 on the entry and another $100 on the exit?

You're in the business of buying and selling stocks not running down petty thieves. Even the time for the back-office staffer charged with documenting the process will cost you more than you'll hope to recover. With the exception of a very few headline cases where an enterprising attorney may have pooled together a class action suit resulting in multi-million dollar penalties, almost no one ever bothers with enforcing the restrictions on front running.

And even if an attorney gets a headline case now and then, the cost to the front runner is usually no more than a few million dollars, but the profit is every day, of every year. The High Frequency trader isn't just making a little amount of money on you. They're making a miniscule percentage of everything on everyone, to the tune of 40% all trading volume.

If this reminds you of that line in the movie Goodfellas,

you've probably got it right. To paraphrase, "There is a lot of money moving in and out of the stock market and they are going to try to steal every single penny of it." They're so good at it in fact, that it makes perfect business sense as mentioned above, for a firm like Robin hood to simply sell them their market flow for a fixed fee and charge their customers no commission. Then Robin Hood has the marketing advantage of no visible direct cost to their customers, while still collecting a portion of the money extracted from them.

Take note. I'm not saying it isn't wrong, or it isn't morally dubious or I approve of the process. What I'm saying is that to most people with a successful trading business, it either doesn't or shouldn't matter. And even if it did, there is virtually nothing you can do about it. If you're of a mind to form a new regulatory policy which finds a way to prohibit the practice then maybe you should think carefully about what else your new policy will do. Policy directives always have unintended consequences.

High Frequency front running is itself, an unintended consequence of the existing policies designed for market fairness which puts the interest of one group of investors against the interests of another. And any new policy that you were to create will absolutely cause a different unintended consequence.

There are far more ways to break things than fix them, so I'd argue that the consequences of your new policy will in all likelihood be worse for investors, not better. More to the point, the regulation came first. The whole HF industry grew up specifically to exploit the gap created by the way the policy was designed. You might not like it, or be happy about it. But broadly speaking it makes business sense to leave well enough alone.

It also makes perfect sense for E-trade, Vanguard, and Interactive brokers to sell their trade flow just like Robin Hood does. It also makes perfect sense for Goldman to give their internal HF market making team first cut at your trading volume and to execute it in their dark pool when possible.

For orders executed against dark pool volume they get a commission from both the buyer and the seller, plus the high frequency skim. The same is true for JPMorgan, and Morgan Stanley, and anyone else you're using as a broker. And because of the natural inefficiency of the enforcement process and the various interests of the market participants, in the overwhelming majority of cases they are going to get away with it. But even if you were omniscient and you changed the rules, the industry would simply find a similar way to get around the new ones.

The practice I mentioned earlier of using the confirmation receipt for the order instead of the order itself, was taken from real life. I was working as a Portfolio Manager in a very large hedge fund when one of our Prime Brokers asked to come meet with us about a partnership they were hoping to create. The Salesman from the Prime Broker proposed that very tactic, along with 10 or so others, all of which were of debatable legality and ethics. His proposal was that we put up the capital, and they will write and run the code, splitting the profits with us.

To the firm's credit, not only did we immediately tell them that a partnership like that wouldn't be in keeping with our firm's ethics, after thanking them for coming by, my boss immediately went to our equity execution desk and had them pull 100% of our execution with that Prime Broker, and begin the necessary custody changes to move our capital away from that source. Instead of getting a lucrative new partnership with a legendary hedge fund, instead they got egg on their face in the industry, lost a big customer, and the salesman probably had some serious explaining to do.

I'm sure that broker met with several other hedge funds, and I doubt they all said no. Since that time, several banks have paid small fines for front running their clients in the dark pools, so someone, somewhere probably said yes to them. And the profit generated by that strategy may have been a nice retort when that salesman's boss started asking questions about why they lost such a high-profile customer like the fund where I was working.

In 2019 according to reported claims, Citadel, the leading high frequency trader in the equity and options marketplaces, extracted 3 Billion in profit from high frequency trading. Most of it, without ever holding a single share of stock for longer than a few milliseconds. No one will ever prove it, but it's hard to imagine that didn't happen without a little bit of front running.

But it honestly shouldn't matter to you. If you do things right, they'll extract their profit from you, and you will extract yours from someone else. Your only goal should be in figuring out who that's going to be. At a certain level, this is what 'information advantage' means.

Another common practice that's a bit more brazen with regard to the ethics of market making is the concept of running the stops. A Stop order is an order to sell at a price which is lower than the current price. The order only goes into effect after the stock price has moved below it, so comparatively unsophisticated investors sometimes use them as a tool for risk limitation. You buy the stock at 100, put in a stop order at 90, and the worst-case price shouldn't be too terribly much below that when your order is executed, giving you a maximum loss of something close to 10.

The practice fell out of fashion with institutional investors long ago since they were only minimally effective during period of high volatility, which is when loss limitation is most needed. They were more or less completely eliminated for institutions when quantitative risk controls became standard in the industry in the 80's. "They don't work, so they don't get used." At least not by institutions. But even during periods of normal volatility the few retail investors who still make use of them provide an opportunity for malfeasance at the exchange.

The practice of running the stops involves two or more floor brokers working in tandem. The guys on the exchange floor are all friends, and sometimes family. "One hand washes the other" was never a great challenge for them.

The market maker responsible for managing the order book would alert other brokers of the prices and volumes they held for stop orders, then quickly move the market down through that price, activating the orders. They would let their compatriot pick off those orders at a low price, and in an instant, move the bid-offer market directly back to the original range where the existing order flow dictated. The accomplice then had shares held at a price substantially below the market, and would sell those shares back to their market maker accomplice at the higher price.

To the investor it would look like the stock price dropped suddenly, their shares were executed at a lower price, and then the price returned to normal. It looks that way because this is exactly what it is. But the challenge for enforcement is still substantial since the practice involves an informal agreement between parties that no one was ever going to be stupid enough to confess. The person who knew where the pricing of the stop orders was wasn't the buying party, so there was never any clear connection to ill-gotten gains.

If you think about the original purpose of a stop order, it was a solution designed to meet the needs of a trader who only had a limited amount of attention. He could buy some shares, put an order in to manage his downside, and move on to thinking about other opportunities. These days, technology has more or less made the entire purpose of a stop order moot, certainly for institutions. But the exchange keeps it in place anyway. This is partly for legacy reasons, but a more cynical analyst might believe the order remains in use because it's a nice source of revenue for market makers, as new retail traders are forced to relearn the lessons of trader's past.

While the quantification of finance has all but eliminated some forms of broker malfeasance, it has created whole new ones that would have been impossible before.

Owing to the severe time constraints imposed by their business model, most high frequency systems aren't so computationally intensive when compared to the systems being applied in longer frequencies of investment. They're super-fast, faster than most people believe is really possible. But that speed comes with comparatively extreme computational limits, so many of them aren't particularly complex. Not much information changes at the sub millisecond frequency. So, they're limited to analyzing just a few dimensions of order flow, and their predictive power is limited to a very short forward-looking window.

There is a wide range of different systems of course, and for the best (most profitable) systems, only the people who have developed them really know specifically how they work. But there isn't much data to look at in the window of time that they hope to predict, so there is only so much they can be doing. For them, a faster forecast is more profitable than a better forecast generally speaking, since it offers more of an opportunity to lock in riskless trades.

One dataset that's been examined carefully by market

making systems, is depth of book. Imagine the best bid and offer for a stock is 45.99 – 46. A one cent bid-offer spread on a 46-dollar price. Under equity execution rules, that bid and offer must be for a round lot – 100 shares minimum. But suppose the offer of 46 represented an order for 1,000 shares, while the bid of 45.99 was only good for 100? That indicates that there is an order imbalance, and it will take a lot more money to move the market two cents in one direction than the other.

Those are also the highest bid and lowest offer. In the exchange order book will be other orders at other prices, representing other volumes. Bids may for example span the gap between 45.01 and 45.99 with 45.99 being the highest. The inverse could be true on the offer side. Those orders won't trade so long as another order is closer to the best market, but prices move. And if the sum of the volume on one side or the other is considerably greater, that will impact price velocity in the immediate future. Orders which are "away from the market" also stand a good chance of being cancelled, so to HF systems, they exist only as probability distributions. "Schrodinger's Volume" is a lighthearted phrase sometimes tossed around among quant teams. Like the similarly named cat, this volume is both there, and not there simultaneously, and only assumes one state or the other when you try to execute against it. These days the lifespan of the average order is measured in milliseconds.

The systems monitoring depth of book, like all market

making systems, are fast but computationally limited. And this is what creates the incentives for the phenomenon known as spoofing. The goal of spoofing is to indicate to the systems that monitor the depth of book that there is more volume extant on one side of the market or the other, without ever putting any actual capital at risk.

According to the regulation, spoofing is very explicitly described as entering orders which are never intended to be executed. Since this distinction includes the concept of intent, under many circumstances it can be very difficult to prove. Like most of the malfeasance that comes from the exchange, High Frequency systems did not invent spoofing. It has a long and storied history and as you can imagine, has seen widespread, but mostly un-litigated use in all the markets.

High Frequency systems may or may not have democratized the process, as they've done with front running. Unfortunately, I have no specific information to confirm or deny this. But it's certainly a reasonable bet that it's occurring frequently in the options markets, as it has always been. These days, with such a short average lifespan for an order, it stands to reason that the lower liquidity markets like the options market would see the practice in more common use.

Many efforts to limit spoofing have been proposed in recent years and the self-regulatory bodies of the exchanges are currently mulling them over. The regulators are well aware that regulatory policies all have unintended consequences, so they're trying to be very deliberate in deploying any changes.

But if you're going to manage billions, then you should learn to look at the regulations in a manner similar to the way that most institutions do. The letter of the law is where enforcement occurs. And though the intent of the spoofing law is quite clear: "only orders which you truly hope to fill should be entered", that isn't what the regulation actually says. If it did include the principle of hope then it would make the law even more unenforceable than it currently is.

So, let's run through one idea, that for the right investor, might represent the creation of an information advantage. One which respects the letter of the law for this domain, but is institutional in its treatment of the spirit of it. The goal here would be to give you a window into the institutional thought process with regard to regulation. This idea has obvious limitations, but it's the closest thing to a potentially untapped working trading strategy that you're ever going to read in a book.

Suppose you were building a day trading system which looked to capitalize on price changes of just a few minutes. When ranking stocks, the order interest (those stocks for which there are the most orders) is Pareto distributed. The most heavily traded names are also the names that attract the attention of the most sophisticated high-frequency systems. But even less frequently traded stocks have market making systems engaged in tracking the bid offer spread. Very few names are managed by discretionary market makers anymore.

In this example, we're interested in those stocks that attract relatively little order flow, making them less appealing to the most sophisticated systems, but still trade enough to justify automated market making. These market-making systems will not be the fastest, or the most computationally efficient. And these names trade so little that the best HF teams won't see much value in trading them. There isn't enough overall volume to make their application worth the investment. In this case, it might be possible to use those system's weaknesses against them.

Suppose for reasons other than the bid offer spread, you've already taken on a position in a particular stock. You've held it for a time, and you're now looking to exit your long positions. Your position is small. Smaller than your individual position limits, so if you were to buy more shares, you would have a greater risk, but not be violating any other normal risk management constraint that your system employs. The stock has seen order flow which is about normal for the name, but compared to heavily traded names, that normal is very low.

If you were to enter a sell order, a normal market making system will attempt to move the bid offer lower, keeping your shares from executing until it can find lower priced shares available on another exchange to sell to you. But what about if you placed another bid to buy more shares? Theoretically, you could enter a bid which is far enough below the current market so that the market maker doesn't simply lower the price and execute your shares, but by entering the order you are increasing the order imbalance, indicating a greater volume of buyers than sellers.

In certain circumstances, this may have the effect of encouraging the market making system to raise the market price rather than decrease it while it looked for cheaper shares. If the market moved the price up and away from your order, you could then theoretically cancel that order which is now further from the current price, and follow it with another order, still some distance from the current best bid-offer but somewhat higher than your last, causing it to move the market even higher. The size of the order would have to be small enough so that if you get executed you can take the shares. But in some lightly traded stocks it doesn't take much.

This does not qualify as spoofing because you are willing to accept the orders if executed. It is perfectly legal to do this in every way, so long as you are prepared to accept the shares in those circumstances where your order is filled. It's simply an attempt to set up a new set of probabilities for exploitation that use the weakness of the market making systems against themsevles.

On the winning side, you have the probability that the market making system is slow enough and poorly designed enough so that it will react to your addition to the order imbalance by moving the market away from you (increasing the profit on your already existing position), measured against the losing probability that you will push the system too far and your order is filled. If there are other orders than yours in place that are away from the best bid and offer, it might even increase the volume per minute executed, attracting other comparatively inefficient systems that are trying to exploit the trend, driving prices even further.

In terms of how this might be viewed by regulators, there is a risk, though I believe it's a very small one. Since employing this strategy will no doubt involve being executed from time to time on your buy orders, it should be easy to demonstrate your willingness to accept the shares. And since your intent is a component of enforcement and in taking the executed shares you're demonstrating your willingness to do so, there is a perfectly justifiable cause to say that since the strategy is sometimes effective, it's effectiveness has changed your intent to sell your original shares and that you now would prefer buying them (if you have to) for the sake of driving the price somewhat higher.

A strategy like this has the distinct information advantage of operating directly on market impact, so it can't really be back tested. This means that very few other market participants will be willing to try it, and virtually none of the traditionally managed hedge funds will. Large hedge funds delegate strategy design to PM's but there is almost always a 'trust gap' in that relationship, and none of them will allow a strategy to be employed without back testing. This strategy can't be back tested, so it's an assurance of at least some exclusivity. If it does work in any systemic way, you'll probably be one of a very few people doing it.

Commit a small amount of capital to testing the constraints and identifying the relevant probabilities, and I may have just given you a multimillion dollar per year trading strategy. One that should have a relatively stable lifespan since it involves a considerable degree of exclusivity.

This isn't going to be a 'billion-dollar trade' idea, but as far as I know, it is an untapped one. It will be constrained by comparatively low volume, and thinly traded names. But there might be a genuine opportunity in it. If it works, I can see a small firm getting a million or two per year from this practice with only an absolute minimum of regulatory risk.

But the real point of this exercise is to demonstrate how institutions sometimes think about wedging their trade strategies in between the regulation, the incentives, the hard limitations of volume over time, and the capabilities and efficiencies of others. It's akin to evolution finding a niche to exploit, in between the optimizations of other organisms.

Find the weaknesses of others models, build a system to exploit them profitably. Do this enough and it starts to add up. A few million here, a few million there, and soon you're talking about real money. This is just one simple example of one potentially productive way to think about it, that's typical among institutional players. It involves nudging right up against the regulatory limits of what's allowed, but not crossing over the brightly lit line that would bring an enforcement action.

Brokers offer an enormous number of services for hedge funds. But on the day to day transaction level, most of what brokers want to get paid for is doing as little as possible. And in truth, once you get past the level of traditional retail brokerage, they aren't paid all that much for doing it. Listed commission for prime brokerage isn't typically a big money maker for brokers. Most people including me, will argue that there is enough competition to keep prices competitive given the risks and effort expended by the banks.

As technology made its way through the various trading services, equity systems have all been automated and the broker staff trimmed. What took 80 people per shift in 1990 when I was at JPMorgan, can now be handled on a twenty-four-seven basis, by a team of less than 20. Decimalization of stock prices allowed for a reduction in the commission rates, and once you make the step from retail brokerage to Institutional prime brokerage, most services are offered on a cost-plus model so there is a very low and completely transparent markup.

The way a cost plus model works is over the years, legions of investment bankers have picked apart the services that the banks provide and the costs associated with each of the people and systems used to provide those services. These cost attribution models have a single goal – to determine what the differential cost is on a client by client, trade by trade basis, in such a way as to give those salespeople responsible for attracting new hedge fund clients a simple metric for determining whether the new hedge fund client will be a net gain or a net loss for the broker, on a fee generating basis.

Most prime brokerages have worked that model into a few simple barriers to entry. The first is a total dollar value of commissions generated monthly, and the second, is a range of rates per share, which the bank must collect on top of exchange fees. These fees are rarely more than a fraction of a penny and allow for a great many strategies to be workable for their prospective clients.

The major banks, Goldman Sachs, JPMorgan, UBS, Morgan Stanley and a few others, all provide identical services in a very nearly identical way and therefore have very similar basic cost structure to one another so they charge more or less the same costs to their clients. That doesn't mean you can't negotiate something better, but except in extreme cases there are usually bigger worries for you.

As an example of a bigger issue, since 2008, the issue of custody has also become a significant concern, especially once you reach a certain size. When Lehman collapsed, many of the assets held by them for their Prime brokerage clients were temporarily frozen, including all of their hedge fund clients. You might have had a few hundred million in assets at Lehman on Friday, but on

Monday, you could no longer access or trade those positions. In that instance, the Federal Reserve and the Treasury department were quite helpful in expediting the release of those assets, but not until after a great many tense conversations with the various hedge funds took place, and the receiver and regulatory bodies agreed to an extra-legal exception. Many hedge fund CFO's spent that extremely stressful Monday screaming at a great many people.

A more common issue in normal markets has to do with something much less formal. A big part of what makes one prime brokerage more appealing than the others in normal market conditions, is how easy they make it to handled exceptions. Simply due to the law of large numbers, any industry which handles millions upon millions of total transactions every single day is going to have a few errors which need to be straightened out afterward. From time to time an order will be mispriced or some other mistake will occur. When it does, you want the process to resolve it to be as painless as possible. In almost all cases these issues can be addressed without lawyers, compliance offices, or any of the regulatory bodies, and it's usually best to handle them that way if they can be.

But that means a great deal can hang on people's willingness to not make a mountain of a molehill, or to find some discretionary way to settle accounts that can meet with everyone's approval. Because this is so, there are few areas of financial services that depend more on the personalities of the participants and their various relationships than prime brokerage.

If you have someone at the brokerage on the other end of the phone who tends to speaks frankly with you, is generally reasonable and reliable, and who you can trust to do their best to help you resolve a problem, it's usually worth more than a tiny hundredth of a penny in commissions. Cost benefit analysis must be applied to your individual case of course. But the bulk of the hedge fund industry still runs this way. And the reason it does is because in most cases it's cheaper than the alternative. But like all things regarding the brokerages, the upside of a good relationship also has a downside. In this case, the downside is that your broker doesn't just have a relationship with you.

One practice that's been common in the hedge fund industry is what's referred to as shopping order flow. Large hedge funds execute with multiple brokers, and the brokers all offer the same service to those hedge funds in more or less exactly the same way. But one way that brokers can sometimes differentiate themselves from their competition, is by making one hedge fund aware of what other unnamed hedge funds are doing.

If hedge fund A has entered a large order to buy or sell a certain stock throughout the day as a VWAP order and another hedge fund learns of it, the second hedge fund has a meaningful advantage in executing their own orders. Maybe it will be enough of an information advantage to change a decision. If so, then it might lead to more efficient execution and greater profits. The practice of sharing this information is extremely common, and though it's very close to violating the regulations, it's still probably on the legal side of it.

The results of these unofficial information exchanges have had some very entertaining consequences over the years. A first-hand account from a friend of mine who ran global equity execution for a very large fund is a good example. This story is out there in the industry chatter, so I'm not revealing any secrets.

His new boss was hired away from a broker, and as new bosses do, he demanded that the fund now work with his friends at his former employer. The execution team did as they were commanded, but when they placed orders with their new broker, some confusion resulted. On a particular day, a few minutes after they had placed a large VWAP order, one of the junior staffers from that broker immediately called them back on a different line to let them know of its existence.

The dim-witted broker hadn't yet memorized the client code for his new high-status customer, and he was so anxious to ingratiate himself, that he was shopping their own order flow back to them. Naturally this raised legitimate questions about the confidence with which their orders would be handled in the future.

No legal avenues were pursued. There wasn't much point. That sort of thing would only be a cost to both the broker and the client and an embarrassing headline for both firms. And that's the way it often is with ethical issues like these. Where interests diverge, they're diverged.

You could say that there is no honor in institutional trading, though I personally think that's a bit harsh. There are rules, and the rules are adhered to 99.5% of the time, which is probably better than most industries. But it's an intensely competitive domain where every opportunity must be exploited and where profit comes almost exclusively from exploiting other people's mistakes. If you want to survive in the jungle, your claws should be just as sharp as the next guy.

Dark Matter

Talk to a few self-taught retail traders, and you'll hear that all sorts of assets are crashing all the time. For them, if a stock they hold sells off by nearly any amount, and for nearly any reason, they will call it a crash. I've been in circumstances where people came to me saying that in their view an asset was "crashing" three or four times a week - sometimes multiple times per day. This view is a categorical error.

The typical group of most frequent traders for any individual stock are fairly stable, so the incentives around the actions of those investors tend to be relatively stable as well. Given a certain stock, a certain number of long only institutions will trade it, a certain number of hedge funds will do the same, and it will have a fairly stable level of interest from the press and retail traders. As a result, each stock has a range of variance at any observation frequency, which could be described as normal (in the non-mathematical sense of the word).

It's slightly different for all assets, but as a general rule, the behavior of prices tends to be fairly stable and predictable within about 2 standard deviations of the mean.[3] When price changes are

---

[3] The fact that I use different numbers to describe this general range in different parts of this single book, should give you an idea of just how much the actual number is disputed in the industry. This is an extremely broad general guideline, nothing more. The closer you look at this phenomenon, the more dispute there is. Not being too obsessive about what the actual number

small enough to be within this general area, the linear mathematics for statistical analysis tends to be fairly good at predicting their frequency. It's tail events, what the press likes to ignorantly call "black swans", which differentiate asset price changes from normal distributions and where predictive statistics breaks down. But even most of those aren't technically "crashes".

In reality, tail events on any individual asset can be caused by a wide array of information, differentiating them from a crash. One poorly thought through tweet from Elon Musk can cause Tesla to shed billions in market value. While his behavior might not be normal for a CEO with his level of responsibility, his frequency of posting irresponsible tweets certainly seems to be. So, a selloff with this information as a root cause, shouldn't be thought of as a crash.

Crashes are real though. And though they continue to be frustratingly difficult to predict, the systemic causes of a market crash are fairly well understood by academics. They're caused by moments when asset prices fall in a degree large enough to justify a deleveraging of positions by other investors. It's the falling leverage levels across investors that identifies an actual "crash".

You own a variety of stocks including 30% of your portfolio in Apple. Bad news arrives regarding Apple and because you hold so much of it, your total portfolio value to drops 5%. Being a

---

is, is probably be good advice. It's by no means a stable and reliable statistic.

hedge fund, you're using the maximum amount of leverage available to you, but your estimates on how your portfolio will behave over time and that are used to guide your degree of leverage, have all been calculated with linear statistics.

That 5% move in your portfolio constitutes a tail event. Your portfolio value is now below the level required for you to avoid a margin call, so you sell some other assets to reduce your credit requirement. Those sales cause the other assets to drop, and when they do, it causes more selling by others who then find themselves in a similarly leveraged position. They inspire others, and so on, and so on.

It's important to remember that on a collective basis, this isn't necessarily the same as a margin call. The largest and best performing hedge funds trade a wide array of assets, some which offer considerably more leverage than US equities. Though they all use leverage, it's rare that they use so much that margin calls have to be avoided. So, it's their own internal assessment of their risk limitations, and the relationships to other assets as they understand them that's driving their decision. Since no one knows what those specific numbers are but them, this makes the actual amount of leverage out there and the subsequent deleveraging point unknowable to others, and very difficult to predict.

This also means that the most important aspect of a market crash is not what people are doing in the moment, but what they've already done. But for the degree of leverage which was already in place when the selloff began, and the relationship of that leverage to their constantly evolving risk limitations, market crashes would never occur.

When a deleveraging selloff is occurring, there are also all sorts of incentives in the marketplace for other types of investors that offer meaningful resistance to crashes. High Frequency liquidity provisioning for instance, for its many perceived negative effects, tends to have a price stabilizing effect when a broad-based deleveraging occurs. HF systems have an inherent long volatility bias so when the bid on one exchange tends to drop more rapidly than another, they tend to buy the lower bid, sell to the higher, and stabilize the price, marginally slowing the speed of descent. It might not be enough to stop the overall direction of price momentum, but it's well documented that it has a tendency to tap the breaks on the way down.

Their effect can easily be seen by comparing the behavior of the stock market during the 2020 Covid driven selloff when HF trading was prolific, to the 2008 market crash when their presence represented a smaller portion of total volume. Or by comparing either of those events to the last true stock market crash that occurred without any HF traders in 1989. While virtually the entire selloff in 1989 occurred between the hours of 1PM and 3PM, in 2020 markets sold off in a more measured percentage over a period of days. The difference could be analogized as a balloon bursting or slowly leaking most of its air.

The unfairly maligned short sellers also have an incentive for stabilizing the most severe market crashes. During moments of extreme volatility when markets have sold off dramatically, their every incentive is to become buyers in the marketplace in order to lock in their profits and stabilize prices. More short sellers will inevitably mean more buyers during the moments of greatest stress. That governments tend to limit short selling during market crashes is testimony to nothing except the megalomaniacal ambition and economic illiteracy of politicians.

For those interested in a more detailed explanation of the various decision-making errors that occur in the lead up to an actual market crash, I suggest you have a look at the academic literature concerning a phenomenon called an information cascade.

To summarize it very briefly, an information cascade occurs when various market participants ignore their private analysis of a stock price, and instead follow the public knowledge of another trader's behavior. Based on their private research the stock seems overvalued which would make them a seller, but since they also know the public information that everyone else is buying, they buy as well. In yet another real-life example of the pot looking disparagingly at the kettle, this is sometimes called the greater fool theory in the press.

Since their rational decision-making processes are no longer functional, as a risk mitigation mechanism, they tend to shorten their anticipated holding period. If they were using their relatively efficient standard decision-making processes, they should be selling for a month, but instead they will attempt a buy for just a day. This sets up a broad spectrum of actors who are no longer relying on a discreet information advantage to make efficient decisions, and ties the future behavior of all of them, to the public event that occurs when buying stops.

A categorical distinction between public and private information isn't always clear. Past trading price and volume certainly qualifies as public information. Most people would probably agree that technical analysis which is derived solely from that data is also public information, reported in a different format. But what about mean reversion statistics, or descriptions of momentum. What about the Beta factor, or correlations of a stock to its leading competitor, or for that matter any inverse correlation to the 10Y future?

There is no hard and fast rule, but the broad industry consensus for the distinction between public and private data has principally to do with the cost in acquiring it. Private knowledge has a cost, public information, generally speaking, does not. Unrelated data charges taken aside, the higher the cost for the knowledge derived, the more likely it will be to private, and the more generally valuable the knowledge gained from that information will be as a source of predictive forecasting.

Back to actual market crashes. Our trader has performed private analysis, and then rejected the conclusions from that analysis, preferring to follow the public data of what other traders are doing. The problem comes when their anticipated holding period grows so short, that their typical rational analysis period is now longer than the holding period. It may take 2 days for them to make a new rational decision, but instead of being a rational actor for a minimum of 2 days, they're now a potentially irrational actor for just one.

Their aggregate information advantage has been cut to zero. And if things go against them, they can no longer have any rational recourse. Their odds of profit are no greater than their odds of a loss. And the hair trigger response required in their new decision-making paradigm makes them excessively sensitive to volatility. When this phenomenon exists for enough investors, the crash occurs.

But there are other dimensions against which it's helpful to look at the deleveraging phenomenon, because it doesn't just effect market performance during a crash.

You may think the total leverage in the marketplace may tell you something about the likelihood of a crash, and it might. But we know that control of assets is a Pareto distribution, where the top 20% of asset managers by size control roughly 80% of the total dollars. If every investor is making use of 2 to 1 leverage, then the amount of leverage will be Pareto distributed as well. This will be considerably more borrowing in dollar terms than if the bottom 50% of investors were taking 4 to 1 leverage, but it would also be far less likely to cause a crash. The thing we're really concerned about isn't total leverage, but the amount of investor assets that are supporting that leverage. An even better metric would involve the volatility of those assets on the balance sheet.

An investor has a lot of choices when it comes to assets. Cash is considered the most stable. Few things will make the value of cash vary much from day to day. Since cash is a promise from a government and bonds are a promise from a private actor, cash is considered the least risky end of the fixed income dimension. Bonds and other lending paper with longer duration or poorer credit quality are considered riskier, so they return a higher yield. Derivatives are most often optimized to provide more direct access to a dimension of risk so they're riskier still. Because equity prices change more dramatically than debt, they are even riskier, as are the options and futures that are based on them.

We know that rational institutional investors all try to optimize between low risk assets and high-risk assets. Each has their own tolerance for risk, and they optimize their portfolio accordingly. We know that if they're striving for the maximum possible return for their investors (and who isn't) then they will be using all the leverage they can, given the degree to which their assets prices change day by day. This isn't necessarily setting the table for a crash, it's just the day to day use of leverage in finance. We're still setting the table.

Here's another rule for the marketplace that matters greatly here. Or rather, it's a rule for humans that's useful to us when we think about the marketplace. The first person to get a new good idea stands by himself. While it isn't necessarily true in all cases, if we think of it in aggregate terms, we can think of that person, at that moment, as the smartest, or the most knowledgeable.

Let's say the idea is to buy X for some length of time. If it really is a good idea, a few more slightly less smart people will get that idea as well, though since their decision making isn't quite as efficient as our leader, they'll take just a little longer to figure it out. What develops is a curve that isn't too dissimilar to the right side of a normal distribution. One person first, a few more next, then a few more and so on. Eventually we get to the point where we're close to the mean of the distribution – half way more or less, to the point where everyone knows that it's a good idea to buy X for the next N period. Time has worn on though. Maybe since the moment that the first person got the idea, half the "goodness" of it has been worn away. It's still got some upside though, so many more people are now piling on.

At the mean point in our curve, there are still a lot of people out there learning the new idea of buying X. You could say it's not that new an idea anymore, roughly half the people already know it. But it's still a new idea to each of them.

But while the less smart half of the distribution is just starting to buy, that first person to originally get the idea, who was first because he has a much more efficient decision-making methodology, is likely getting a new idea. He already has a position, so his incentives have been meaningfully changed. His idea is that since half the people available have already bought X, maybe buying X isn't that great an idea anymore. Maybe to that person, selling X and taking a profit now looks like a newer good idea.

So, he starts selling, while others are buying. And when we get all the way down to that last person all the way on the left side of the bell curve and the last person available to buy is finally catching onto this new idea that everyone has decided is good, our leader has already sold out the last of his position in X, maximizing his profit and is on to his next good idea. Maximum profit from a single trade can be fairly conceived of as a maximally optimized efficient decision-making process. The last person to figure it out, who has the least efficient decision-making methodology, doesn't do nearly as well.

Let's go back to looking at the degree of leverage. The Norwegian National Pension has 1.4 trillion dollars under management before any leverage is applied. If they were to take on 1 trillion dollars in leverage, in ISDA terms their degree of leverage would actually be quite low.

If that leverage were distributed optimally across all their assets, the odds of them having to sell anything in order to avoid margin requirements or their self-imposed risk limitations, would be basically zero. But for the reasons mentioned above, if you take that same 1 trillion in leverage and spread it equally among the bottom performing hedge funds, there will be more of a risk of deleveraging contagion.

The bottom performing hedge funds manage very little in hard assets each, so it would take quite a few of them operating at the regulatory limit in order to consume all of it. Even the smallest downtick in prices will necessitate their selling something to gain more liquidity. More to the point, the bottom performing tier of hedge funds aren't typically very original, or know terribly much about managing risks, so it's entirely possible that they're all making exactly the same trades as everyone else in a comparatively inefficient way, and relying on being a part of the herd to ensure their profitability.

They believe they're smarter than average, and in truth they may be, when looking at the investor population overall. But that isn't really the question. The question really is how much knowledge about this decision do they have. When it comes to coping with a trillion dollars in leverage, each of them probably has less experience with their portion of it than the Norwegian National Pension would if they used all of it themselves.

So, when the bulk of the leverage is in the hands of efficient decision makers that understand risk, the relative odds of a crash are low. When the inefficient actors are the ones drawing all the credit, the cumulative market sensitivity to leverage is much higher.

Here's a rather extreme example from real life. Sometimes ideas catch on and become contagious. Any idea that leads people to believe they can get rich without the hard work of converting costless information into valuable knowledge, can be especially communicable. In 2008, the contagious idea was that anyone could get rich by buying houses and flipping them. You had people who were of no more than average intelligence, buying multiple houses with high leverage at low teaser rates, and selling them again immediately in order to profit from the asset inflation in the housing market. That worked fine, until it didn't.

In 2007 during the run up to collapse I would arrive at Penn Station every day off the very first train in from the NJ coast. I had been doing this for well over a year, and since I got to Manhattan at about 4:50AM and the streets were largely empty, I always got in the same cab with the same driver. She was a very charming middle-aged woman, originally from Barbados, and in our early morning drives across the empty city, we became quite friendly. She knew my daughter's name and my various parenting foibles, I knew the names of her kids and grandkids and some portion of the drama in each of their lives. I wouldn't call us close, but we were certainly on friendly terms.

Apart from her taxi job, she had also been flipping houses in greater Atlanta, sight unseen. She knew I was in the finance business so she would ask my opinion about it, and I always counseled against it. I genuinely liked this woman, and wished she and her family well. But it was clear to me, as it probably would be to almost anyone, that she was playing a game that she really didn't understand.

In the weeks immediately before the collapse, I left NYC and took a position with another large hedge fund in Greenwich CT so I stopped my morning cab rides and never knew exactly what became of her fortunes. But I think the outcome for her was fairly predictable. I do know in June of 2008 she was supporting 3.6 million in mortgage credit on her cab drivers' earnings of less than 80K per year, and with nothing close to the assets she'd need if prices fell. Most of her teaser rates were due to expire near the end of the year, and when we last spoke, she had already been complaining about the slowdown in turnover.

This was not an immoral or greedy woman who deserved what she got. She was incredibly hard working. She had endured remarkable hardship early in her life, and she remained a cheerful and optimistic person who enjoyed spreading that good cheer to others. All she ever wanted was to make the lives of the people around her better. Her great mistake, if she can be said to have made one, was that she became convinced that there was a way for her to get rich with very little effort. She thought the rules of the game had been changed in a way that made it easier than it really was. And I have no doubt that she paid a high price for this error.

In the housing collapse, prior poor decision making conspired to put a great deal of leverage into the hands of a group of people who understood very little about how to manage it. There was a knowledge bubble. The market structure also played a role, as did the foolhardy and shortsighted political actors who created the incentives both for the banks, and for the borrowers. The incentives worked precisely as they were intended to, but as is all too often the case, the political actors didn't think of the potential unintended consequences of their choices.

Political actors live in a world where you can choose who wins and who loses. Give a benefit to one group and the costs for it to another group. This is how the world works when viewed from Washington. But the financial markets don't work that way. They are inevitably self-correcting whether anyone likes it or not.

Market crashes always involve a knowledge bubble. They involve people who don't precisely understand the consequences of what they're doing, and are doing it anyway because they believe they've found a way to a short cut. They believe they've found a way to get large profits at little cost in time, energy or effort. And they try to do it without the decision-making knowledge required to be considered a rational actor.

Once you've been around enough, you'll see this in a smaller scale all the time in the financial markets. One recent example I can think of involved the uproar in the spring of 2020 around the Reddit "Wall Street Bets" phenomenon. Using the Robin Hood trading app, a bunch of financially illiterate kids were using extreme leverage in the options space in order to squeeze the market makers into moving the prices of thinly traded stocks. For the most part, the kids had no idea what they were doing, and their semi-public tactic of using a Reddit channel called "Wall Street Bets" to share information and act informally in concert, fell outside the regulatory limits of the industry. Collusion is illegal among known parties and is severely punished when proven. But none of these kids knew each other, so their practice fell just outside the domain of enforcement.

It was clear to me as I watched it, that what was forming was a knowledge bubble. They had caught the market makers off guard by working in concert, and since they were informally coordinating, the market makers had initially been taking it on the chin. They would respond to the sudden order imbalance and liquidity shortage created by these highly levered bets by suddenly raising the stock price, and the kids would profit from it by selling out their shares or options when they did.

I knew there was a massive knowledge bubble at work, and the Reddit kids were perversely open about it. They didn't really understand how leverage worked, and they believed it was a one-way street. One they could use to take advantage of others, instead of one that could just as easily be used to take advantage of them. As I watched it, I was confident that it was just a matter of time before more knowledgeable actors began to feed on the kid's ignorance.

Sure enough, after a few weeks the market makers had

figured out their game. When these kids (and I do mean kids, some were 17 year olds lying about their age) would use massive options leverage to create a liquidity shortage in the stocks, the market makers would simply fail to rise to the bait.

Instead of responding to it by letting the price rise as they normally would, the market makers would make up the liquidity difference themselves by taking on additional risk and keeping prices right where they were. They knew the kids were highly levered so time was working against them. All they had to do was hold prices in the normal range for a single day, when mark to market accounting would force the kids to sell out of their highly levered positions to avoid margin calls, whatever the price was.

The result was the kids no longer getting the price spike they hoped for, and the market makers began taking a profit instead of them. Sure enough, in just a few weeks the financial news was populated with kids taking stratospheric losses. And even though it was the result of a simple reporting error, there was even one tragic (but morbidly well publicized) suicide among them which was a product of this craze.

The example I used to describe the market maker squeeze at the close in the "Timeline of a Trade" chapter, is taken from this example. The kids thought they could game the system, and in the end, the system gamed them. What happened to those kids was essentially a deleveraging event, but the only people affected by it were the members of "Wall Street Bets" and the only people profiting from it, were the people they were trying to take advantage of who knew more about how markets work and the incentives of the players, than they did.

This sounds horrible, but the fact is that this is one of the great strengths of the design of the current capital markets. Over the long term, it's knowledge that's rewarded not tricks. Tricks can work for a little while, but there are so many differing interests that there is always someone out there who has a profit motive to keep the machine working correctly. As they say on the options floors, volatility giveth but volatility also, taketh away.

Volatility is very well understood in quantitative finance even if liquidity, which is often the driver of it, really isn't. As I've mentioned, the quantitative finance industry doesn't have a mathematical definition for liquidity. But you don't have to know precisely what liquidity is to know that when all the buyers have all become sellers, a lack of liquidity is exactly what you're going to get.

And since no one tracks liquidity in any cogent way (there being no cogent way available yet to do so), and there is no way whatsoever to predict it, in many cases it's easy not to notice it or to ignore what might happen if it were to change suddenly. This error can have catastrophic consequences. The unforeseen consequences always look the same, as do the kinds of errors that lead people into these traps. And it isn't just retail investors who get themselves in this kind of trouble. Sometimes the only difference is in the sophistication of the error.

Shorting Volatility

Macro traders tend to focus on big trades that usually take a great deal of time to develop. The information advantage they typically look for is one created by an uninformed politician, the generators of a monetary policy, or some other macroeconomic policy error in a big liquid market. The biggest winners tend to be on the long volatility side when liquidity shortages come into play, and everyone else is in a panic. The movie "The Big Short" highlights a set of people who were successful in this class of trade.

Their big trade was caused by a macroeconomic error that almost everyone else made in the 2008 housing crisis. Specifically, the error was the belief that the market for mortgages was ruled by local economic conditions that were not nationally correlated. Housing can collapse in Detroit while Palo Alto booms. This was in fact the case for most of our history.

But when the government created a set of unified national political motives for writing more mortgages for low income households, Federal regulators had given all the mortgage writers a shared set of incentives. Being rational actors in aggregate, those incentives caused them to all behave the same way. Over time, this caused markets that were located far from each other to become correlated, for exactly the same set of reasons. And by transferring a huge amount of leverage to people who really didn't understand it, it exposed that entire market to a massive liquidity risk.

This wasn't highlighted in the film. The movie focused solely on what the "bad guys" were doing and what the "heroes" who guessed right had done. That's half the story. But the banks, like everyone else, were only doing what they were incentivized to do. The government chose the music, and the banks did their best to dance to the mandatory tune – the same as they always do.

The traders featured in the movie had identified a set of circumstances which they believed would result in a collapse of liquidity in mortgages. Subprime loan writing for people with poor credit had exploded nationwide, and this put the bonds at risk of collapsing all at once. Given the mammoth size of that market, they all knew it would be bad, but since liquidity isn't quantifiable, they didn't know precisely when it would happen or how bad it would be. In the end, they were right to varying degrees, and huge gains were the outcome. But even in the movie, that wasn't without it's stresses.

Few people from outside the hedge fund world probably noticed a moment in the film where Dr. Burry was leaving his office and wrote a note on his whiteboard indicating that his fund was down 19.7% - just 0.03% away from violating his ISDA agreement. This number is branded into the brains of anyone who has ever managed money in a hedge fund. As a kind of mild form of hedge fund PTSD, I gasped uncontrollably the first time I saw it and my heart rate jumped involuntarily. Several of my friends reported the same reaction. For us, that was the very real sword of

Damocles that hung over all our heads, for as long as we did our jobs. That made it a far more terrifying scene for us than any horror film because this monster was real, and it was prowling around out there for all of us.

But for that 0.03%, instead of windfall profits Dr. Burry could very well have had a 100% loss, years of heated litigation, and potentially even lost all his personal wealth. It's happened to others. In the book version by Michael Lewis (but excluded from the film) were several real-life cases of others who guessed right about the liquidity crunch but got the timing wrong by just a little, and were ruined in the process. That scenario matches my recollection of events as well.

You can think of that dramatic drawdown as essentially being the same thing that happened to the kids from "Wall Street Bets". The only difference was that Dr. Burry was either correct or lucky with his timing, and was saved from what was in effect, a kind of margin call. But it was easy for even professional investors to lose sight of the chances they took with liquidity for all those house flipping home owners. Things in that kind of market environment happen very quickly. And unless you're very thoughtful about the risks you're really taking, the things that are happening, could very well be happening to you.

Back in my research days, one of the functions of my role was to help discretionary traders who were in a slump, to apply quantitative discipline to improve their performance. I was working at a top tier hedge fund, so the discretionary traders I was working with were some of the very best in the industry. A few were true legends who had made billions in profits and hundreds of millions for themselves. These were experts. The best of the best. But even in that environment, I saw one particular class of error from them that was terrifyingly common.

At one point, I had been asked by the big boss to work with a currency trader of some industry renown. He is just about the nicest and most generous guy I've met in 30 years in finance, so I won't name him, but anyone in the industry would certainly know who he is. In the 80's and 90's as markets became globalized, he made a fortune trading currencies. Currencies were booming then and less experienced traders were entering a market that he already understood very well, so he took great advantage of their relative inexperience.

But by the early 2000's the Euro had been established, and the big currency trades of the prior period had largely quieted down. Central banks had begun communicating with each other and coordinating their actions. And when volatility in the market dropped as the pricing of new information became more efficient, his P&L slowly declined.

He wasn't losing money, he was just treading water. And it had been a while since he had a really big profitable year. That can be tolerated by a hedge fund for a good long while when you're a well-known name like him, with a breathtaking lifetime track record. But no one wants to live with performance like that forever. This is when I was asked to advise him on how he might improve his odds.

When I met with him, the view he described went like this. He felt confident that his understanding of his markets was such that he would be in a position to identify a big price move if the circumstances to create one emerged again. In his mind all he needed, was a means to generate a small amount of profit on a monthly basis, in some steady quantitative way. His thinking was that he could do this with a carry trade, which works like this:

One country posts a 3-month risk free rate (for example) of 0.05% and another, say an emerging market country with much worse credit and higher inflation, posts another of 0.11%.

You borrow money for three months in a low interest rate country, for example by selling a 3-month US T-Bill short with extremely high leverage, and you then lend the money received in that transaction in the emerging market by buying their 3-month bills. At the same time, you effect a 3-month currency forward agreement, hedging yourself against currency changes by locking in the rate at the current price. You then collect the difference in lending rates. You're paid every day for 'carrying' the trade on your balance sheet.

In this example, a fully hedged 100 million-dollar trade in risk-free or fully hedged assets would generate a 60K profit, more or less. When performed at the maximum degree of leverage, this takes less hard cash than you probably imagine.

60K isn't a huge gain on 100 Million for three months – just about $1,000 in mark to market profits per day. But if you do it often enough and with enough leverage, it starts to add up. Remember, his goal wasn't to generate 'knock it out of the park' performance. His goal was to juice his returns by a small amount per month while he waited for the big trade he imagined was going to come along eventually.

What hadn't occurred to him was that the whole reason he wasn't seeing big trades any longer was that the currency markets had radically improved in efficiency. New information was being processed by the most efficient actors almost immediately, and by nearly everyone else soon after. There was no longer a big information advantage to be had like there was when new uninformed players were entering that market. By then even the least efficient actors had radically improved their models and increased their decision-making efficiency.

But with that said, his thinking for a carry trade was sound, so I sat down with a programmer and designed a system for him that would allow him to monitor and trade the carry on a variety of markets, including the Indonesian Rupiah.

He traded the system for a few months while he waited for his big trade to arrive, and he made a small amount of money with the system, just as he intended. In fact, the longer he waited for his big trade, the more it began to look to him like there might be more of an opportunity trading the carry than he thought.

Yes, he could make an additional 6% a year or so, and that certainly met his initial goals. But he soon discovered that he could also look for some higher paying opportunities. Places where the yield curves between countries were offering serious premium. He could imagine a circumstance where he might be in a position to trade some very large positions (all fully hedged) and make a double digit return on carry alone.

This is the point where the clever reader will notice a similarity in his decision making to my friend the cab driver. Even though he was a much more sophisticated investor than she was, he had convinced himself of the same delusion. He believed he had found an easy way to make a lot of money at very little risk or cost. He believed he was fully hedged. He believed the rules had changed and he had found a flaw in the system – a magic formula. All he had to do was make what to him was a relatively simple transaction, and wait.

But here was the rub. These positions were hedged, but not against everything. The borrow and lending contracts were both fixed, so they were OK. The forward rate agreement was fixed, so it was OK. There was a minimal amount of counterparty exposure in sovereign credit, and he was dealing with tier one banks, so custody wasn't a major concern (this was several years before the Lehman collapse amplified custody risk in people's minds).

But what he didn't count on was the political risk associated with dealing with third world nations. Just after he increased his exposure in Indonesian Rupiah to a much higher level than he'd ever previously done, the Indonesian central bank unexpectedly devalued the currency which changed the notional amounts on the Indonesian side of his trade, leaving him exposed to the tune of several Billion notional dollars (not cash), in a market that was now moving strongly against him, while currency traders tried to get a handle on the changes.

What he hadn't figured (In spite of the fact that I mentioned it continually while building the system for him) was that a Carry trade is a bet on things remaining the same. It's a bet where you are paid for the passage of time. And all bets of that type are Short exposed to Volatility in some way. The euphemism for that risk position is picking up pennies in front of the steam roller. And in this case, the Indonesian steam roller, rolled right over him. By the time he netted out his additional exposure, he had lost every penny he had made since adopting the strategy, and a bit more besides.

You hear about blow ups from shorting volatility all the time. They tend to have large numbers associated with them, which tends to attract the ghoulish press who love nothing more than to giggle over the carcasses. Several of them have been very public. Long Term Capital Management got caught out on a short volatility position. Amaranth Capital Advisors did the same. So did Bear Stearns and Lehman. It's a fairly common error that's always made in a similar way. All of these blowups are driven by a sudden shortage of liquidity.

It's worth mentioning the LTCM case briefly, just for its level of sophistication. Economics Nobel Prize winner Myron Scholes, a name that's treated with deity like reverence in the derivatives markets, was a key architect in that blowup. His intelligence is really beyond reasonable dispute. Even his market knowledge was deep and considered. Yet his firm still took one right between the eyes in a liquidity crunch, very nearly collapsing the entire US economy in the process.

In that case they got caught in a liquidity squeeze between on the run US Treasuries on one side and off the run Treasuries on the other. Most readers have probably never even heard of the difference. An oversimplified example is that if you want to lend money to the US government for 2 years by buying the debt, you can buy a newly issued 2-year note (an on the run bond) or you can buy 5 or 10-year bonds that were issued years ago, with just 2 years left (the off the run bonds). Since the on the run bonds are most often the cheapest to deliver, they are easier to hedge in the futures market, which makes them more liquid than the off the run paper. And bonds aren't like stocks where one is the same as the other. With bonds, there is a specific set of cash flows representing a specific numbered Bond.

The moral of the story is that Myron's undisputed intelligence didn't help him, and your intelligence won't save you.

As I've said countless times now, success in this field has only a little to do with intelligence. Everyone in quant finance is a genius, and if you're still considering getting into it, then you probably are too. But the thing that has the potential to make or break you isn't your intelligence. It's your ability to manage your own psychology, and to overcome the traps that your own brain has set for you.

The psychology of a trade like this is always the same. It involves someone who believes for whatever reason, that they can get paid without taking on risk. They enter the market with something other than complete knowledge, and those unaccounted risks, inevitably come back to bite them. The risk is there. It's always there. The only real question is whether you see it or not, and are doing something rational to address it.

The Billionaires you admire all see it. Paul Tudor Jones came to fame by predicting the 1987 crash. The stories aren't as well known outside the hedge fund world, but Izzie Englander has a dozen scalps on his wall from smaller liquidity crunches that didn't make the headlines. Louis Bacon made huge money on the Russian Bank Crisis, on Turkish Lira, and dozens of others. Whatever you think of him as a person, George Soros was so good at exploiting these opportunities that he very nearly bankrupted the Bank of England, who had put themselves in that same awkward position.

Every one of them is looking for the same thing. The place

where people believe they're smarter than they really are, or know more than they really do. They're looking for knowledge bubbles. Places where people believe that making big money has become easy. Places where people with little actual knowledge, think the world has changed and they've found a new secret. Those people are all making errors. And the billionaires of the hedge fund world, are all prowling the markets every single day, looking for ways to make them pay for their hubris.

I have one caveat to add here. Unlike all the other views I describe in this book which are a reflection of well-established industry consensus, I have a personal bias against shorting volatility that is not universally shared in the industry and my accounts reflect that bias. Many allocators will feel exactly as I do about it, but a few won't. There might be room for reasoned debate about it. None of that changes the fact that it represents what is so far, an uncontrolled and unquantifiable risk.

For me I believe there is a question of ethics involved. If you run a short volatility strategy that will pay you year after year and then in year five, loses six years of profits, making your total net gain negative, you still got paid for five years. This logic is more than enough to induce some managers to pursue it.

I couldn't do it, but I also don't judge. You can form your own opinion about how to approach a strategy which involves it. So long as you go into running such a strategy with open eyes and are fully transparent about it with potential investors, I think it will be received about as well as it could be.

Creating an Information Advantage

Information is prolific, and to the rational investor, most of it is useless. It's all around us, all the time. But in the hedge fund world, we're not interested in information. What we're interested in, is usable knowledge. And tragically, usable knowledge, is never free. In fact, in most cases, knowledge is worth something close to what you pay for it, but you don't have to necessarily pay in dollars.

In my house, we jokingly refer to YouTube University as a place where you can learn a minimal level of competence in just about any conceivable human task. And though it's available without a capital cost, converting that information into knowledge still requires payment. You're still going to have to spend the time, energy, and effort necessary to find cogent videos, watch them carefully, and if necessary, follow their instruction.

The same is true in the 21st century hedge fund world. What you're after is knowledge that will give you an insight into the decision making of other investors. In a sense, you're looking to front run the decision making of other investors by anticipating what they're going to do. If you believe they will make a decision based on the announcement of sales data, then you look at information which will give you some degree of insight into what those sales numbers will be in advance, and buy or sell it before they do.

The strategy I designed and ran profitably is a (now dated) case in point. When I started building my news reading system, there were no vendors selling a dataset for news. Reuters and Bloomberg were both publishing news that could be consumed by their subscribers in real time so traders could watch it on their screens along with their charts, but neither had yet built a database where you could get a look at the history, and use it for back testing. In order to create the first version of my model, I was forced to build a routine which subscribed to the news in real time, and stored it locally for later consumption.

The whole process took a little over 2 years to gather the relevant data. And that time commitment made the dataset relatively expensive on a labor basis. Very few people were going to go to the trouble of capturing and storing that kind of information when there was no proven value to it. Since I went to the trouble, the information had a relatively high information value, and when I built a fully automated system to execute against it, I had an instant information advantage over other market participants.

In just a few years both Reuters and Bloomberg had made changes to their systems in order to make their news database available for a fee. A great many more people were willing to pay a fee than gather and store the data, which brought more competitive players in, and lowered my information advantage and my profitability. I made another time investment by changing the analytic and hedging dimensions of my model slightly, and as a result remained profitable. Soon after that, they also made the data available for others to rebrand and resell at an even lower cost, bringing even more players into the space and making my information advantage even smaller. Even more changes extended the profitability a bit longer.

Because it operated on the news in a manner which was different from the kind of sentiment studies that others were doing, it continued to remain profitable for a total of seven years. It probably would still be profitable today if I restarted it. But the strategy had a long volatility bias, so over time the volatility of the P&L rose so much that it was no longer profitable enough on a risk adjusted basis to justify a 2 and 20 fee structure, and I could no longer think of new ways to improve it, so it was retired.

The point is, scarcity of data can provide a meaningful advantage to you if you can process it in a way that gives you an insight into trader's actions, that few others are willing to pursue. Exclusivity if you can manage it, is a sure-fire way to increase your odds of an information advantage.

As another example of exclusivity of a dataset, let me go a bit further back. In the early 2000's I was still working in research at a major hedge fund, and we were asked to participate in a data study that was being run as a partnership between MIT and State Street Bank, the massive Boston based trust custodian. The MIT team had produced a dataset by taking the gazillion small currency transactions from the massive pool of small trusts where they were custodian, commingled them together by currency pair and date, and then obfuscating that data into a set of time series of Z-scores to preserve anonymity. They then gave the data to the research units of a few key banks and large hedge funds for analysis, to determine if there was trading value in it. I had a relationship with the MIT team at the time, so my team was one of those chosen.

In many ways, this was the perfect predictive dataset. Since MIT and State Street had decided to keep the data exclusive in order to maximize their revenue from it, very few people could get a copy. Only 5 or 6 multi-billion-dollar global hedge funds and a few big banks even knew of its existence.

Even if someone else had heard of it, the pricing they were proposing made it wildly expensive, and that was a big barrier to entry as well. Only those very few funds who had the capital to exploit it fully, would bother to do so. The data detailed currency transactions, the single most liquid market in the world. It was delivered on a 4-day delay – meaning that since it took some time to settle transactions which were being rolled up into the dataset, the information delivered on Thursday would be the transactions record for the previous Monday. When it was first delivered, the data was preliminary and not final, so It would continue to be updated for four subsequent days, when the final numbers would be released.

My team looked at this data very carefully. We looked at it across currencies, across forward dates, across the update periods of observation, and across various predictive lengths. And we determined that under certain circumstances the data had a breathtaking predictive value.

Under certain conditions, it was a better predictor of 3 month forward rates in certain currencies, than any other information commonly available. Given the liquidity of those markets, one could very easily build a model using this data alone, and make several billion (with a B) dollars per year at full liquidity capacity. At those numbers, even if we could affect positions with no more efficiency than the other half dozen hedge funds that were also seeing the data, we could still expect to make hundreds of millions per year.

If you were in a similar situation, what would that data be worth to you? You're already a part of a business designed to trade currencies in large size, and with fairly good efficiency. You have the balance sheet size and credit available to accommodate the risk. You have the traders, the counterparties, the systems, and the staff to manage settlement and clearing. You need only build a system to manage the regular delivery of the data, parse it into a model, run the model at a given frequency, trade the result, and collect the money. Hundreds of millions in additional profit, within a very well understood risk dynamic.

So, what's the data worth? A couple of days non-recurring

programmer time aside, your only new cost is to buy the data for X and you then collect Y, where Y is greater than 250 Million dollars a year. Would you pay a million dollars a month for that data? How about 10 million a month? I'm not what anyone would describe as a great mathematician, but it looked to me like we could pay 10 million a month and make 20.8 million from it, every month. Would you take that deal if it were offered? Suppose your odds were less than 100%? Would you do so based on a probability? How sure would you have to be that you're going to collect 20.8 million, in order to be willing to pay the 10 million data cost up front?

In the end, it didn't matter. That dataset was never released commercially and we never got the chance to actually buy it (we'd have happily done so). But this data story provides a great window into how to think about the cost of knowledge. And it has all the important components that analysts looking at Alt-Data should be cognizant of.

For starters, it was difficult data to get. You had to be in the right kind of firm, and even then, you had to know the right people. If data is seen by fewer people, all other things being equal, any value that's teased out of it will be of greater monetary worth, and with fewer people looking at it, it will take longer for another team to expose the same information advantage. Compete with one other market participant and all other things being equal you'll split the total alpha two ways. Three participants, three ways, and so on.

Lots of things that aren't quite as obvious as this MIT example can make data difficult to get. If a dataset starts as a widely distributed disparate dataset like social media posts, then only those analysts with the resources to manage that will have it. If it takes some higher mathematical function written in some dynamic new way in order to reduce the lag the data is reported on, that can help also. If you're asking a counter intuitive question that follows a chain of logic most people won't, then that may be an advantage even if access to the data is fairly prolific. You may be utterly wasting your time, but if you aren't, then you'll be more likely to have the information advantage all to yourself.

In essence, the more of an information cost you pay, be it in cash up front or in systems and analytics in order to accurately process it, the fewer people in the marketplace who will be willing to go to the trouble of doing so as well, and the less direct competition you'll have. The MIT data was very expensive compared to most currency data, and since it took the combined resources of both State street and MIT to distill it down to a usable format, it was more precious still.

State Street had already made the decision to limit the scope of its release of the data, restricting it to the biggest players. That limited the effective dissemination of the data even further to only those players who had the confidence in their own team's analysis. Believe it or not, large hedge funds usually view their own team's new research with the same cynicism that they attribute to outsiders. And if it isn't already apparent, a fairly high degree of confidence in a quant team needs to be a pre-existing condition in order to get someone to pony up 100 million per year in data fees. It should go without saying that unless the fund is directly committed to quant trading like Bridgewater, DE Shaw or Renaissance, this circumstance is not a common one in the hedge fund world.

The model my team used to expose the predictive value in the data was not mathematically trivial, so it also required a PM who felt confident in their own quantitative skills in order to understand it. Few billionaire hedge fund managers (or investors in general) are prepared to listen to a story that to them sounds like, "I promise I can make you a fortune doing this complicated thing that you don't understand, and it will only cost you 100 million a year in unrecoverable costs to see if I'm right." I can only imagine the reaction had I tried to convince my boss at the time to go with this argument.

This is an example taken from the extremely high cost end of the spectrum when it comes to the idea of generating an information advantage from data. But there are equivalent examples at the low end of the spectrum. And this brings us to another rule enforced by the incentives in the marketplace that are a product of the continual pressure placed on institutions for generating profits. One which the more quantitative among you should take very, very seriously. Low cost of information, in the end, is equal to low information advantage.

Many readers might find this discouraging, but technical analysis costs almost nothing. There are hundreds of books in every free library detailing how the analytics are derived, and they cost virtually nothing in terms of data and systems time to calculate. Some retail brokers will provide a basic set of analytics to you free with their software. It's so low cost that it isn't completely clear that it's private analysis at all.

Do technical indicators work? Well firstly, is that the right question? That's a binary question with a binary answer. Binary questions don't apply well to population data, and we know that in trying to model decisions, the best questions are those which produce a distribution of results. Maybe a better question would be one where our results can be tabulated as a distribution … say… "Under what circumstances do they work"?

The answer, which is probably obvious to many, is that yes, under some circumstances and absent any other market effects, they can offer a degree of predictive value over some relatively short time frames. In terms of assessing the behavior and decision making of investors, there are some small investors and floor brokers who still use those indicators as primary buy sell signals. To the degree that they do, and in moments when absolutely nothing else is happening, technical indicators can be useful.

But they can't do very much. Their predictive value is so

low, and of such a short duration, that they can be very easily overwhelmed by the effect of other actors using other signals. If a large seller arrives in the market for whatever reason, any technical buy signal will be negated for the duration of that selling pressure. If new news breaks immediately afterward, it has the potential to negate any buying pressure created, and so on. Yes, they drive a tiny amount of behavior in a tiny portion of the tiniest of the capital markets, specifically equities and crypto. They might even be an even tinier portion of the larger futures markets. But putting your faith in technical indicators alone is rowing into a very big ocean in the tiniest of boats. If anything at all happens anywhere else in the world, the boat will capsize, and you're going to the bottom.

But if your business model is structured correctly, then technical signals shouldn't necessarily be totally ignored. If for instance you know you can react to the technical data faster than other market participants who are also using just that data to generate signals, then you potentially have a meaningful advantage over those specific investors, however much volume they generate. If you are disciplined about it, you might also be fast enough to get out of a losing situation as well, before it does much damage.

As mentioned in other sections, there is always someone who is faster. But your goal isn't to be fastest overall, but to be faster than those who are attempting to predict similar time period as you. To the degree you're fastest among those, you'll be taking their money, instead of them taking yours.

But from the perspective of an institutional investor whose confidence you require for your success, it's difficult to imagine them finding that story compelling, when your real advantage is your skill and speed at execution.

There are better examples of how the cost of the knowledge you get is a pretty good proxy for the advantage it will give you. In the social media example that I used to describe Market Efficiency, everything in the Ad market was based upon the ability to predict ways in which large groups of people are similar in their decision making. Most of that description is probably pretty intuitive.

But why are the decisions of people who are engaged in the financial markets any less predictable? There are fewer of them than there are people seeing online ads so the sample sizes are smaller, but their decisions and subsequent actions are also much more frequent, much more deeply constrained by incentives, and the constraints upon them are much more easily inferred from their choices. They aren't announcing their choices on social media, but maybe there are other ways you can derive an estimate of what they do.

Take the example of a large asset manager who runs a long only strategy – like Berkshire Hathaway. Due to their larger size, they will typically take days to enter or exit a position, and the methodology most frequently used will be some version of VWAP – an execution algorithm which attempts to deliver a filled price which is equal to the volume weighted average price on a given day.

They don't much care whether they're filled at the bid price or offer price at a given moment. Given their specific execution goals, it represents too small a portion of profits to make it worthwhile to invest too much in technology to solve. VWAP, for them, is a kind of optimization. It's good enough due to its very low relative cost. This means that if you can successfully predict when Berkshire Hathaway is either buying or selling, you could theoretically capture a portion of that bid offer spread as profit when their excess selling temporarily drives prices down, or their buying, up.

Berkshire Hathaway also isn't the only long only fund out there. A great many other businesses run long only funds (or long short for that matter) with similar constraints on their decisions. In fact, a great many of them tend to think, like those Ad buyers, in very similar ways. It stands to reason that if they're in an efficient market like equities, their decision making will be both inspired by and constrained in similar ways. Berkshire Hathaway might be better at it over time than some similarly constrained actors, but is there any reason to believe that they'll be that way every time?

Suppose you discovered that some other long only fund manager – BlackRock for example, was better at managing their interest in the transportation business than Berkshire and tended to react to the same kind of new information that Berkshire does, but did so in a slightly more efficient way? You could then follow Blackrock's activity, and use it as an opportunity to predict the future behavior of Berkshire, buying in the market at a lower price that does not yet reflect the Berkshire interest.

To be perfectly clear, these examples are fictional. I have no idea if BlackRock and Berkshire have any interest in common, or in truth, whether they actually run their businesses in the same manner in any way. I'm using common names only for the purpose of illustrating a point.

The point is that to the degree that market participants are running similar businesses, their activity in the marketplace will be similar. If you look at that interest on a time-zero basis from the point at which a new piece of information arrives for processing by market participants, their interests will be a bell curve shaped distribution. The fastest and most efficient actors will act first capturing the greatest profit from that new information, and the least efficient acting last, capturing the minimum profit or maybe even taking a loss.

Let's take the example from the other end of the speed spectrum, the high frequency market makers, all of whom have similar constraints and incentives. The perfect trade for all of them is one where they buy in one geographically distant market while selling in another at the same moment in time, and capturing a price differential. That is a riskless trade, but it isn't without costs. Everything is always a Swap, so there is a cost side and a benefit side. In this case the cost is the expensive technology required to perform that trade, and a sizable investment must be made in data and system costs before the first trade ever occurs.

They know about the distinction between normal distribution similarity of decision making and Pareto distributed differences of all market participants – in most cases they live and die by it. And they all start from the same perfectly riskless starting point.

So, let's suppose we wander from the perfect and identify a set of trades where they can do the same thing, buying in one market and selling in another, but there is a one millisecond difference in time. That would mean that they are holding long or short, some portion of stock, for 1 millisecond. Their risk in that trade is the amount by which the price of the stock held will vary, in a single millisecond (actually it will probably be a reduced order fill rate). Not a huge risk perhaps, but not zero. It's probably best described as a probability itself. And differential risk probability is the core of their game.

If it can be made to work for 1 millisecond, how about 2 milliseconds? How about 5? Now we're talking about a very real risk in comparison, where a meaningful portion of stocks will move in measurable amounts or the volume is captured away by others, leaving them holding a position. And they need to conceive of this risk as a matter of cost and benefit – like a swap. Does the probability of positive cash flow (a profitable trade) adequately compensate them for the probability of a negative cash flow (closing their position at a loss due to price change over time?) If the answer is yes, then of course they're going to make the trade.

Think about the ways you can look at that trade. Differing stocks will all post differing probability of a price change over 5 milliseconds. Which stocks and how much? The more liquid stocks will be available more frequently so the amount of the price move over 5 milliseconds will be probably be smaller on a price basis. But being faster is an absolute distinction. It doesn't matter if there are 10 people and you're the fastest or if there are 100 people and you're the fastest.

Stocks with less liquidity will typically have a larger bid offer spread and require a larger price move to eliminate the risk. Even the dimension of stock price comes into play. Higher priced stocks will represent a greater dollar value of risk for the same number of shares, while lower priced stocks will be lower dollars.

But all the right questions and all the right answers always comes back to those two distributions. The Bell Curve, and the Pareto distribution. Some better mathematicians than me will certainly quibble at this point about the precise nature of those distributions, and they do so to their credit. If they can say things about that distribution shape which are more precise than I do here, then they have used their superior mathematical knowledge to generate an information advantage, (over me at least) and the hedge fund industry will be very interested in hearing any evidence they can provide to support their claims.

Let's take that example even a bit further. What else do the HF market makers have in common? Well one thing they all have in common is that they are operating on very short time horizons, and that minimum amount of time imposes its own serious decision-making constraints. There are for instance, only so many calculations that the bleeding edge technology can make in a single millisecond. How many? I have no idea, but I know it's finite even if it's theoretically changing over time in accordance with some derivative of Moore's law.

But suppose the technology reaches a point where some mathematical benchmark was struck. Suppose the barrier for accuracy in prediction could be greatly increased using a differing method, if only that method could be reduced to a process which requires only 1 millisecond or less, in a way that couldn't work with the previous technology. Suppose it could be rewritten in a differing language or by some new mathematical formula or derivation. Maybe bringing in quantum machine time will be a key. That will have a cost. Will it also have a quantifiable benefit? All of these breakthroughs represent meaningful profit opportunities to a HF market maker, and will no doubt be a part of their ongoing research. As such, they could be an opportunity for you if you have the right skill set.

Let's look at that a slightly different way. Rather than a technology optimization, let's look at a business optimization. Suppose a HF market maker knows that at 5 milliseconds, they are currently at a break-even probability on the majority of stocks, using their current technology.

Their technology isn't designed to make use of the 5 milliseconds, it's designed to be optimized for 1 millisecond. 5 is just the probabilistic limit of their current, even higher speed forecast.

But suppose some other team within the same parent organization has built a system which will hold stocks for 3 minutes on average, and be wildly profitable on its own using completely different analytic methodology. Their calculation takes much longer than 5 milliseconds, but once every 30 milliseconds or so, it will go into the market, and buy a list of names to hold for those three minutes.

Now suppose you're a firm like Citadel, who also runs a very substantial hedge fund that engages in investment on all sorts of time horizons. You know that every 30 milliseconds, there will be an increase in buying pressure for a portion of the stock held in risk by your HF market making team. When that happens, the buying pressure created will push the price in a direction that your HF team finds useful for generating profit, changing the distributions difference between your profitable trades and your losing trades for the HF market making team. In essence, instead of having to wait for the signal of that order imbalance, the HF team can anticipate it owing to their knowledge of the activity of their other internal teams.

These companies may be under the same banner, but they are actually two differing companies, one making markets, and the other speculating. So, in a circumstance like this, there will be what's called a Chinese wall between the two companies, which prohibits the sharing of information or intent. These Chinese walls are a common practice in Investment Banks and always attract careful examination from market regulators.

But in a highly technical high-speed world, there is more than ample opportunity (ethical or otherwise) to obfuscate the transfer of that kind of information. The firm can, in essence, shop its own flow from one area of the firm to another area, giving a pricing advantage over others to the HF team at a negligible cost to the low frequency team. The net effect is for the HF team to take profit from their direct competition in the HF space, while having no real effect on the longer holding period strategy, which would have been paying that money to someone either way.

Let's say the regulators decide this is against the rules and fines Citadel for doing so. As a whimsical and purely theoretical example (I have no evidence that this occurs, but it wouldn't shock me if it did), rather than giving the HF team access to the buying and selling info directly from the hedge fund side of the Chinese wall, the HF team monitors the chip temperature of the computer systems the hedge fund team is using. They can correlate that information to changes in overall market activity, exposing the data from the hedge fund side. They could in theory even pay the hedge fund side a fixed fee for this temperature data, sharing a portion of the profits generated with them. Both teams overall generate more total profit, and Citadel the parent does even better as compared to its competitors on both sides.

Will a move like monitoring chip temperature be allowable by regulators? I don't honestly know. Those regulatory decisions always involve broad discussions of intent and effect. But the questions you have to ask yourself in determining whether the regulators will allow it is really this:

Can the justification of the practice be described in a manner that eliminates the obvious advantage, and who will have a better understanding of the data used to justify the decision, the practitioners or the regulators? They could theoretically claim on the HF side that they've determined that there is some spurious correlation of that information for reasons unknown, and since no specific trade data is being shared, it shouldn't fall within the bounds of regulatory scrutiny. This is the domain of lawyers and outside my expertise. Much more likely is that they'll fail to mention it at all and make the regulators both find the signal and prove there's something inappropriate about the transfer.

Even if the regulators do eventually eliminate that option for allowing the market making team access to the information, how much of a fine are they likely to incur? Is that probability of penalty lower than the probability of net profit after fees to the parent company before the regulators disallow it? If the answer is yes, they're going to make the trade. Why in the world wouldn't they?

And going even one (slightly ridiculous) step further, let's assume that even a blind squirrel finds a nut eventually and the regulators inevitably expose the breach in the Chinese wall. If and when that happens and the regulators impose a fine and order the data sharing ended, there will still be other more cleverly obfuscated opportunities.

The HF market making team could, for example, make a switch to monitoring their own chip temperature, and the hedge fund team's computer will just have to be moved to a position beside it in the rack, so that the market makers will only have to deduct their own chip temperature activity from their numbers, before coming up with a corollary of outside temperature to represent the hedge fund's activity.

Is this actual optimization happening? I have no idea. I did say whimsical so probably not. Even I think this is taking things to the limit of extremes. But if you want to see if it is, I'd suggest looking for evidence in the market for a sudden price rise of ultra-high sensitivity thermometers used for chip temperature in and around Chicago.

The point is that this is a common way that the industry

looks at these opportunities. Finding that kind of wiggle room between the efficient business models of one market actor and another, or between the letter of the regulation, and the spirit, are all a constant and eternal part of the process of producing a reliable profit in the hedge fund industry. Anything less is choosing to be a less efficient decision maker. And instead of being the diner, you end up becoming the dinner. We only eat what we kill. Even if the only thing we kill is each other.

Right now, someone is making a mistake. They're buying or waiting when they should be selling, or selling when they should be waiting or buying. It truly doesn't matter that they're all geniuses, or legends and they've been doing this for three decades. They're all wrong a meaningful portion of the time – everyone is. All you really need to do is find a circumstance where you can tap the right kind of information at the right speed, and the right time, so that you're just a little less wrong than they are.

Cognitive Concerns

In spite of being surrounded on all sides by competitors large and small, some with what can fairly be described as vast resources and circumstantial ethics, the person who is going to work the hardest to prevent your success in the financial markets can be seen every time you look in the mirror.

All of our brains are the product of hundreds of thousands of years of natural selection, in an environment which has virtually nothing in common with the path required to be successful in trading. And to be successful, unless you're one of those exceptionally rare creatures who comes by it naturally (and you almost certainly aren't), then you're going to have to learn to think differently.

I'm convinced that to un-train your brain, and shed the philosophical and psychological processes which all but ensure your failure, is the hardest task before anyone looking to reach the pinnacle of the hedge fund industry. It's so difficult, I'm not certain it can be performed as an act of will at all. It's entirely possible you either have it, or you don't. At a minimum, I think it's safe to say that it's beyond the capability of most people, however intelligent they may be. I can say with 100% certainty that what I'm talking about is completely independent of intelligence. In fact, this is the very reason I've repeated that axiom so often.

Anecdotally speaking, I'd say more than 50% of all people will lack the necessary cognitive discipline to even begin this discussion. If you read this next section and come away believing that this has "nothing whatsoever to do with trading" or that it "certainly doesn't apply to me", then you're very likely one of those people.

Of the others, most will strive to achieve it and fail. I can't count the number of times I've watched it among my peers and employees, or found an ex-post example of it in myself. I've watched brilliant analysts spiral down a couple of common intellectual rabbit holes in spite of any and all advice, more times than I can count. It's been the most heartbreaking portion of my career.

If, however, you can see some virtue in trying to understand the way your own mind conspires to prevent your success, then in my estimation, the door is at least open to you. You might not be able to navigate these paths right away, or you might not find my description of them particularly useful. So be it. They're certainly not the only description.

But if you can get to a point where you can recognize that these limitations aren't just "other people problems" and that they probably refer to you in some way too, then I think you've greatly increased your chances of success. Add your already established outlier intelligence, a strong work ethic, and a big dose of humility, and I'm confident you'll be much closer than most.

I'm going to do my best to give you one description of what this internal mental process looks like. It is by no means the only way to describe it. One thing it certainly is not, is a complete description. But I spent my entire career working for men who were able, via nature or nurture, to crack this nut, when almost no one else I've met in my life has been able to.

Pick the name of a hedge fund legend. I am completely certain that whoever it is, they've found a way, either internally or externally, to solve these common cognitive problems. It's a thing that the successful all have in common. It may, in the end, be the real answer to 'how do I become a hedge fund billionaire'.

Reason vs. Inspiration

One of the most interesting aspects of human cognition are the contradictions. Those who are incapable of honest introspection are also incapable of even the most rudimentary self-diagnosis – even of their own lack of honest introspection. Most people agree that we live in an age when lying in public is more brazen and more obvious than it's been in the past. Everyone is certain someone is lying, but there is a great deal of disagreement about who that someone is. The gap between those two views comes from the differences in two modes of human cognition.

At every step and in every decision, the process of finding a pathway to success in trading requires continuous doubt. Doubt of others sure, but more importantly doubt of oneself. There are no questions which can be dismissed as being so true that they don't require evidence. And having found evidence, it's a subtle distinction to know when that evidence is enough. Nothing in the hedge fund world is ever really considered proven until you've consistently made the trades, taken all the money, collected all the fees and cashed the check. In some cases, even that isn't enough.

This is a question which revolves around the cognitive methodology we each use to determine the truth. There isn't just one pathway to that category of idea in the human mind, broadly speaking, there are two that concern us. And the opposing methods are the principle source of the conflict about who is lying, and who is not.

Fortunately for us, the question of how we determine what the truth is has been considered by other greater minds than mine. One such person from history whose categories for truth I find very useful, was a 13th century Sicilian monk named Thomas Aquinas.

Aquinas was by any thoughtful account, a very clever man. If you ask the folks in the Philosophy department of your University of choice, it's quite likely that they'll tell you he was one of the greatest minds in the history of western civilization. But like all great thinkers the point he made was actually very simple and in some respects made by others before him as well. I seriously doubt that he realized he was actually describing what psychologists sometimes view as two differing modes of human cognition, but that's turned out to be the case.

His great claim was that there are two ways that a person can find the truth. Aquinas's two identified paths to truth were via reason and revelation. He was making the seemingly obvious claim that you can in fact figure out what the truth is, by looking at the world around you. In 13th century Europe, this was hardly settled business. At that time, ideas like magic were still a comparatively well-respected category, worthy of serious consideration. The witch might not have been "real" to our use of the word but the fire they were burned in certainly was, so a great many people were utterly convinced that magic was real.

The base assumption by the ruling authority of the day, was that the people have no idea what the truth is nor any functional idea how to find it, so they should be told what to think by their betters rather than being allowed to come up with it on their own. The prevailing argument that Aquinas was offering opposition to, was that truth could only be arrived at via revelation from God, which in 13th century Europe meant, via scripture.

In our secular world, you need to step back a bit from that phrasing to truly understand how it still applies to modern cognition. The word revelation doesn't work very well in a mostly secular society like ours. In its place, let's use the words inspiration, since the meaning is pretty much the same. In terms of cognition, what I'm really talking about is the difference between a truth supported principally by belief, and one which is supported principally by doubt.

Inspiration works like this. The truth is revealed to you. It can come to you any number of ways, but you're certain it's the truth. You can describe it as a spark of creativity. You can describe it as a deeply held feeling. You can describe it as your personal truth or your vision. It doesn't matter. All that matters, is that this truth arrives in your head more or less fully formed, with very limited input from the outside world. Maybe you've seen a single anecdote that supports your view, and without bothering to examine any other evidence, you've declared this to be the 'truth as you see it'. Your confidence in this truth is absolute.

As I said, the source of this inspiration isn't really important for our purposes. What is important is that once this truth is revealed to you, being a thoughtful person, you set about trying to validate it as you would other ideas. You take this truth as it stands, fully formed, and go out into the world to look for evidence which supports it. What you do is technically called rationalizing. External validation of your already established truth comes to you because you seek it, and having sought it, you find exactly what you're looking for and nothing more.

For inspirational truth, the process then stops. You have the truth and you have evidence. No further consideration is necessary. If there is easy evidence to contradict your view, it can probably be explained away. There is no reason to look for any counter-factual. On the contrary if anyone else presents one, it will seem distasteful or disloyal to you in some way. From the moment you embrace it, your confidence in this truth is defined by your belief in it.

On the opposing side of this 13th century debate was Aquinas's reason. "Truth" said Aquinas, "can be found by observing the world around you." You look at the myriad of categories and contradictions in the world and try to derive rules explicitly from that information which seem to illuminate some aspect of the phenomena you see around you.

Unlike inspiration, reason uses doubt as its fundamental

basis. "Does this rule hold true in all circumstances?" In the modern world, the idea being validated is sometimes referred to as a hypothesis or theory. And as the world is examined further, and more information is brought into the validation process, the theory can then be changed or for that matter totally refuted, in order to incorporate the new information.

The reason these two categories of true ideas matter in trading because of their comparative reliability. Revelation or inspiration, can be critical in making personal and deeply subjective decisions. But reason tends to be a much more reliable (and therefore successful) method of determining the truth of objective phenomena like the financial markets.

The really slippery cognitive issue though, is that even when we're dealing with purely revelatory truths, they look perfectly reasonable to us. Our mental categories for true and untrue are much more brightly lit than those which describe the methodology we've used to determine them. For a great many people, even some extremely intelligent people, just identifying the line between the two modes of thinking is completely beyond their capability.

Right now, at least a few people reading this are saying *"This doesn't apply to me, I only ever use reason."* You're absolutely wrong. I have zero doubt (irony noticed if not fully intentional) that in a 10-minute conversation with you I can expose a nearly limitless number of places where your "true" ideas are supported by your belief in them, rather than any bottom up factual assessment of the world based on doubt. They have to be. This is a basic part of the design of human brains and is true for all of us.

I've had these conversations countless times, and it's never failed. Others, most annoyingly my 20-year-old daughter, have done the same to me. I'm not exempt either. This is a feature of human cognition, not a bug. It's simply the way our brains are wired.

Ideas which have come to us from reasoned truth and inspirational truth are all tangled up in our brains. It's all a twisted mish mash categorized primarily into true and untrue. Until you've practiced it, it's not at all a simple thing to tell which method you've used to come by these truths. You're far too accustomed to testing them solely for falsehood, and it takes quite a large number of mental calories and quite a bit of self-discipline to do anything else.

More to the point, that a truth came to you via inspiration doesn't necessarily make it less true. It only means that the cognitive method you're applying is less reliable than others available to you when examining objective phenomena, and you shouldn't use that kind of thinking if you can avoid it, when designing a trading system or wondering how to trade.

It's a tragic fact of human psychology that it's comparatively easy to determine whether someone else is engaging in rationalization rather than reasoning, but damned difficult to figure it out about ourselves. Everyone believes they're being reasonable even when it's obvious to virtually all external observers that they aren't. Self-Assessment has an incredibly poor track record in cognitive science, because the inner landscape of our minds conspires to hide our lack of objectivity from us.

Walk into a crowded sorority, point at a shadowed corner of the floor and loudly say "Look, a mouse!" How many reasonable reactions do you think you'll get? Count them. How many people do you see who think they're being reasonable? Count those. How much do you want to bet there will be a sizeable gap between those two numbers?

Here's a more applicable example. Get a large group of people together picked at random, and interview them one at a time. Ask them this one simple question. "How smart are you?" You will get answers which range from "very smart" down to "about average". Some will give you an IQ number. Those that do are probably lying and adding something between 5 and 40 points.

No one will go any lower than "about average". Even people who are obviously less intelligent than average will never assess themselves that way. Technically of course, half of the people on the planet are below average in intelligence. As an external measurement, human intelligence falls on a bell curve. But taken as a self-assessment, it usually produces a Pareto distribution. The important takeaway here is that this is a phenomenon that applies to all people, sometimes, and in some ways. There are no exceptions, including me and you.

In trading, the problems this causes can be manifest in a few different ways. Think about the design of computer trading system using alt-data. The designer has chosen a basic information model as well as a series of tactical methods for exploiting market inefficiency. To use my own example again, let's assume that this system reads the news and trades the resultant stocks, while incorporating a hedge designed to mitigate Beta effects.

The basic information model is that news is the initial catalyst of price movement. This may be true absent all other macro inputs in the stock market. But what happens if the markets begin to react to a larger market phenomenon like a change in interest rates? On a normal day, the effect of an unchanged interest rate is tiny compared to news. But when interest rates change dramatically, their effect on equity market can be enormous. The equity market is too small to handle the massive capital flows that can result from a change in rates, so stocks can sell off or rally dramatically in reaction to it. In that environment, news can mean very little for the price of an individual stock.

In my case, the tactical tools the system used were all derived as a product of reason. We examined the yin and yang of liquidity, the range of normal market behavior and employed a tactic for hedging away normal beta. I understood the question and how to structure the answer in the markets, so the hedge worked very well so long as market behavior remained in the normal range of motion.

But during periods of deleveraging, liquidity takes on a larger role, and the Gamma associated with stocks won't be consistent. The hedge was designed to reflect a historic correlation between the stocks, but during a dramatic enough selloff the correlation of all stocks increases eventually to one, and the hedge would be insufficient.

In those circumstances, comparative headlines aren't going to matter much, and the hedge will probably need to be adjusted, putting us in the circumstance of selling the hedging instruments into a falling market. Using standard hedging strategies, I had a system which was going to be correct and profitable according to my expectations in 99.9% of all circumstances. But because I had looked at the problem in the right way, I was aware of the effect that falling liquidity would have and I incorporated it as a factor when selecting a hedge. So even in the .01% I was missing, the adjustments required would be minimal.

But suppose I had come by that information model using inspiration, and instead of subjecting it to reason, I really and truly believed that the difference between stocks was a function of their comparative differences in the news. Suppose I firmly believed that sentiment was the primary driver of stock prices, and instead of using reason to doubt and test that assertion, I instead spent years trying to validate my inspirational claim that sentiment was the ultimate driver of price behavior. Mine was not a sentiment model, but let's suppose it was.

In that "true" circumstance, there would be no need for a hedge at all. In fact, the cost of the hedge might seem like a big negative. If I knew the truth in my heart of hearts, there would be no need to hedge. Macro market changes are about currency, fixed income, and futures. I'm not trading those. I'm trading equities. So, I don't have to worry about those parts of the market that I don't really understand. What I understand, and know the inspirational truth about, is equities, and that truth revolves around sentiment.

That rationalization I just wrote was paraphrased from a friend of mine. He said more or less that very thing to me, so it's another real-life example of a real-life belief in inspirational truth over reasoned truth. He's one of the smartest men I know, and he still had no idea what I was talking about when drawing the distinction. Sharper minds build more complex traps for those of us trapped within them.

So, here's the real question regarding how this esoteric concept can make you waste time and money in trading. If I had built my strategy that way married intellectually to my basic ideas about sentiment, when that basic information model failed as it would during a market crash, would I be willing and able to surrender my core belief in how markets worked? Could I give up on what I saw as my great intellectual breakthrough and deal with the world as observed instead of continuing to try to rationalize my inspiration?

Maybe. But maybe not. Painful losses are often an excellent teacher and the source of much humility, even if it arrives a bit later than one would wish. But it's at least possible I would remain ego wedded to my model, resulting in a dramatic loss.

Instead of stepping back and identifying my own error through doubt and humility, I might instead have spent my time trying to tweak and tune my model to identify the moment when sentiment had turned against me. Even though it's well known and well tested fact that crashes don't come from a change in sentiment. On the contrary, they usually occur when sentiment is very near to universally positive.

So, in the face of the well documented unreliability of self-assessment, how do I really know if I'm engaged in reason, rather than rationalization? Design of a trading system can be a very complicated and layered thing. So how can I trick my mind into determining that I'm approaching it in the right way at all levels, to ensure the highest probability of profit?

One really clever idea that's been put into very famous practice in the hedge fund space is the idea of debate. No one knows everything, and if you're reasoning, then discussing your ideas with others can only help you. The process of reasoning is improved by discussion with others who offer differing viewpoints from your own, and reveal aspects of your question that you wouldn't otherwise see.

Ray Dalio has very publicly embraced this external solution

for validation of ideas. His managerial concept of "radical transparency" is sometimes misinterpreted as a political power play – making the little guys expose all their best ideas so they can be exploited by their bosses. But that's not how it's intended at all. The goal of "radical transparency" is to subject everyone's ideas to debate and the reasoned criticism of others, regardless of their rank in the firm. The top guys all have to subject their ideas to review, even by the little guys.

In a setting like that few inspirations supported only by rationalization can endure. And clever man that he is, to be sure the process didn't get too corrupted by petty differences or personalities, the process Dalio laid out for his firm involves not only criticizing the offered idea, but criticizing the critics to ensure that the points they raise aren't a product of their own inspirational belief or some vindictive personal attack.

But there are limits to public validation as well. In abstract, if you get a group of people together who think the same way, share the same values, or are possessing of a common insecurity, they can often come to the same rationalized judgements in common. This happens in the political decision-making sphere all the time on both the left and the right.

Social pressure is a well-known phenomenon in the political domain, but it doesn't just effect what people say they've decided, it also affects the methodology they use to decide. In a setting where public validation of ideas is the rule, evidence, especially contradictory evidence, needs to be given a much greater weight. And additional doubt should probably be the rule when it can't be reconciled.

Remember, crashes occur when the majority of people all miss the pre-existing risk at the same time. They all march forward thinking things will remain the same just a little longer. So, like mindedness and any assumption held in common, is worthy of much suspicion. If a sentence starts with "We all know that...", the very first question should be "Do we all know that and if so, how?"

For the more emotionally disciplined among you, there are other internal ways you can figure out if you've arrived at a revelatory or reasoned truth. One way is to monitor your own reaction to your ideas being doubted. If it makes you angry in even the smallest amount, it's a revelatory truth. Call a tall man "shorty" and he will not be angry, not even a little. He'll probably just be confused. That lack of emotional response indicates that his ego isn't vested in any way in the criticism. He isn't sensitive to it, so he doesn't react to it. The only criticisms that ever make us angry are those which we believe contain at least some small element of truth.

Which isn't to say that controlling your emotions is the same thing. All people are, in essence, emotional decision makers but some of us are more emotionally disciplined than others. To truly test your own brain for the means by which you view something as true, is a task which can require spectacular mental discipline.

And in my case at least, I think it's a very subtle distinction between controlling a small emotional reaction, and having none at all.

I'm going to mangle the technical psychological language here toward the goal of clarity. A reasoned theory or hypothesis can be imagined as a kind of external thing. It's not as closely held to us as a revelatory truth which might be better described as a vision. A hypothesis doesn't make us special in any way by our knowledge of it or belief in it, and it's divorced from our egos in a way that a more closely held subjective truth derived from inspiration never could be.

I have another quick story which stands as even greater testimony to the importance of making sure your ideas regarding the markets and trading are as divorced from your ego as they can possibly be. This one comes from my old boss, Paul Tudor Jones. But to properly understand this story involves imagining what the life of a billionaire must be like.

If you're a billionaire, you can have anything you want. Anything. You can surround yourself with sycophants who will tell you absolutely anything you want to hear. Want to declare up to be down? No problem. People will line up for the privilege of agreeing with you for a price that you absolutely can afford.

Paul was never interested in that sort of thing. Instead he valued people who weren't afraid to disagree with him. He was less worried about them being right all the time than he was with them being honest about what they thought. He wasn't a passionless unfeeling robot, quite the contrary. But his lack of emotional response to any reasoned market disagreement was legendary.

During my tenure at his firm, there was an internal chat system that could be accessed by portfolio managers. I was monitoring it one day when a conversation about gold was taking place. Paul made a comment that he thought gold would be an excellent buy over a specific period of time if a specific event occurred. Immediately a response flashed up from one of my peers. He was a PM, just a PM. Not some senior staffer who had been with the firm for years, just another guy who managed some money – somewhere between 100 and 400 Million, just like me. His exact response, directed at Paul, on the public chat which was available to every financial decision maker in the firm was: "You're out of your fucking mind."

Had someone spoken to Louis Bacon that way, it would be easy for me to imagine them leaving the office by way of the 53rd floor trading floor window. One of the many things a billionaire can afford to buy is mandatory good manners from those around him. Had they said that to Bruce Kovner, I believe he would have frowned, excused himself from the discussion, and then his operational minions would have spent the next few weeks making sure the offender was unemployable in any industry, and ruining the man's life in every conceivable way. I thankfully lack the imagination necessary to picture the future horror that awaits the first man to treat George Soros like that.

Paul was a billionaire just like those men. He could afford absolutely anything, including having the man's body disposed of in some impossible to detect way, while he lounged in a public setting with lots of witnesses. He'd never even consider it, but he could afford the price if he did. He could destroy the man, the man's family, and everyone he's ever met, and still have enough money left over for several private jets. He could wipe the man's existence from all human memory, all the way down to deleting his school records and his birth certificate. This guy had just profanely trashed Paul's view in front of dozens of witnesses. No billionaire has to take that kind of disrespectful treatment from anyone.

Paul's immediate response flashed up just as quickly, and was simply: "we'll see." I don't know this for certain, he was out of my line of sight at the time. But I'll bet he was smiling when he typed it.

He couldn't have been thrilled about the tone, but he wasn't going to make an issue of it. He understood that people disagree in good faith, and he was so practiced at keeping his ego out of his decisions that it never even phased him. And there is a vitally important lesson in his complete lack of emotional response.

That information exchange was a product of one of the swap trades that Paul had personally made. He traded away the possibility of his own hurt feelings and having everyone defer to his legitimately unrivaled authority, in exchange for the increased likelihood that he was seeing the objective truth in the market, and hearing other honest informed opinions about it. That sort of thing happened at his firm because he wanted it to, and he was prepared to pay a price for it. The knowledge it gave him wasn't free, but he could still afford it. I don't think that's a coincidence.

When it comes to rationalizing, this kind of reaction is impossible. If you've embraced a revelatory truth then any challenge to your idea is seen by you as a kind of heresy – literally a lack of belief. You'll see it as a deviation from the known truth you already hold in your mind. You'll almost certainly have strong feelings about it, even if you know how to control those feelings. And you'll probably think less of the person who advocated any doubt, in some small way. This is a feature of human psychology, not a bug.

Unlike what you may have learned from watching Star Wars, in trading you want to very much distrust your feelings. Your feelings will only ever lead you away from the objective truth, and toward a truth that may be important to you, but has no place in finance. The goal is to avoid as much error as possible. Reason is a far more reliable method of getting there.

The Dunning Kruger Effect

As I said, we all live in an age of lies, even if there is no clear consensus about who is doing all the lying. That lack of consensus is a product of our differing modes of determining the truth. We all use both methods sometimes, and for some topics. And since it's become a recognizable feature of our time, some of the more technical phrases used to describe the various errors have begun to work their way into our common understanding as well.

You hear the phrase cognitive dissonance all the time these days, mostly from people who don't know what it means and are in all likelihood guilty of it themselves. Another phrase you'll hear is the Dunning Kruger effect, which seems to be gaining in popularity as an insult if nothing else.

The Dunning-Kruger effect is the term coined to describe someone who is so incompetent that they lack enough knowledge to understand that they are incompetent. That may be harshly worded but that's unavoidable. Phrasing it any more gently makes the point within too easy to miss. But here's the really harsh portion of it. This phenomenon, where a person lacks the knowledge necessary to understand their own incompetence, applies at some times and on some subjects, to very nearly 100% of the human population.

The most effective approach to avoiding Dunning Kruger is

to approach all topics, even those where you feel you possess real expertise, with a degree of humility. Trading is not a domain of absolutes. Nothing is ever fully known in trading, there are only topics where the supporting evidence to date, far outweighs the contradictory evidence.

With the possible exception of those phenomena which have reached the academic status of laws (like Gravity, or Supply and Demand) you should never be so vested in any idea that you aren't open to hearing evidence on the other side. Einstein's theory is still called a theory. If enough appropriate evidence is brought to light refuting it, it will be tossed on the intellectual ash heap along with humors, or astrology.

It also helps to remember that though we spend an inordinate amount of time trying to determine causality in finance, the things we identify, even those that prove successful, are by no means permanent. The incentives in the marketplace change over time in response to regulation, politics, and many other influences. So, to be an expert last year may in fact mean that you're a comparative neophyte this year. It can happen. You should be open to it. Which is to say that far more often than not, revelatory truths are typically the domain of Dunning Kruger.

It's really just sloppiness of language, but we tend to believe that "smarter" is a bigger differentiator than it really is. A better way to look at it, particularly in trading, is 'knowledgeable'. More knowledgeable means more likely to avoid error. Smart, doesn't necessarily get you that. Most people think I'm a pretty smart guy. But there are vast areas of the human experience about which I know absolutely nothing. In those domains, even someone with much less raw intellectual horsepower than me but more relevant knowledge, would be much a better person to look to for cogent advice.

I've been an investment allocator, and I've spoken to many, many others. Dunning Kruger is one of the phenomena they're looking for. It's a great way to get a glimpse of belief in a falsehood, or to measure a person's character. "Fake it till you make it" may be a valid strategy in some domains, but in trading and the hedge fund world, I'd recommend against it. If you don't fully understand a concept, especially early on when you're more likely to be forgiven for your ignorance, you're probably better off saying so.

Early stage allocators will be accustomed to it. If they like your ideas they might be willing to offer help. Some early hedge fund investors even have business models where they expect to bring that to the table. They can give you risk management expertise, help in reporting, operations help, a wide variety of options. In cases like this it's my personal opinion that you'd be better served by exhibiting good character than you would be by faking knowledge you don't actually possess, and thereby being accused of exhibiting the Dunning Kruger effect.

There is another cognitive error that's getting more attention lately, and that's a concept called motivated reasoning. Motivated reasoning is one of the simplest principles in cognitive science to describe, but one of the hardest to understand, and by far the hardest to recognize in yourself. Even recognizing it in others can be difficult, which can make it particularly pernicious. What's worse is that it applies exclusively to reasoning. It has nothing whatsoever to do with the difference between revelatory or inspirational truth, and reasoned truth.

One fairly useful description of it that I'm cribbing from NYU- Stern Business School, Social Psychologist Jonathan Haidt, is that it's easier for humans to reason around the edges of a thesis with which they already agree, and harder for them to reason around the edges of a thesis with which they don't. This seems obvious on its face, but it's subtler than it seems.

Many of our political views are a product of motivated reasoning – on both political sides. You'll sometimes hear people describe their political opponents as dogmatic. This is one way of characterizing other people's ideas which may have a strong connection to motivated reasoning. The political opposition may be pointing to a perfectly legitimate concern, but because the solutions they offer have been derived using motivated reasoning, many people will be unable to approach the idea because it falls too far from an idea they already hold.

As an example, take the issue of income inequality. It's widely agreed that the existence of income inequality is factual. It exists. Jeff Bezos is very rich, while many other people are very poor. And the Pareto distribution of wealth has a greater slope now than it has had in the past. To acknowledge its existence is not to validate any personal assumptions about its vice or virtue that tend to come along with discussing it.

When quantitatively analyzed, it's pretty clear to see that income inequality can lead to social instability, decreased social cohesion, and can reduce the level of social trust in a society. All but the most sociopathic agree that social stability, increased social cohesion and greater social trust are preferable outcomes for everyone.

But since addressing the issue is complicated and the solutions on offer from both political sides are typically the product of motivated reasoning, nothing ever gets reasonably discussed. Each solution presented, represents an idea too far outside of bounds for the other side to be considered a reasonable methodology.

This is not to call one side or the other right or wrong. I have no interest in politics, it's just a useful example. All I'm saying is that since the solutions on offer from both sides are a product of motivated reasoning, the other side isn't willing to entertain them even for the purpose of a discussion.

The way this cognitive error manifests in trading follows a well-worn path. I can't count the number of times I've seen a systems designer build a trading system which tests well and produces profit for a limited time. Then as its performance begins to wane, instead of applying reason and rethinking the base assumptions in the system's design, they will attempt endless fitting, refitting and inevitably over fitting of the existing variables.

As the performance wanes, it then affects the system designer's ego and exposes their insecurity. Their stress level rises, and with it, the odds of a cognitive error. In reaction, they become ego wedded to the basic concept of their strategy, and unwilling to consider that the things their strategy initially got right and wrong, or that the actual concerns to which they should be applying their energy, have changed. Motivated reasoning wastes their time, and the validation they're using for their system makes the jump from reason to inspiration, and down the rabbit hole they go.

One thing I find helpful to think about in a case like this, is that there are three most common modes of failure for a program trading system. If it's a short volatility strategy (Imagine selling close to expiration options for the tiny premium or the examples I listed in past chapters) it will work well for a while and then all blow up all at once – usually taking tons of past profits with it. Liquidity collapses suddenly and the strategy fails. If it's long volatility, then over a period of time the P&L volatility will increase while it gets crowded out by other increasingly efficient market actors with a similar strategy. Liquidity increases and the strategy grinds slowly to a halt. The third is that it simply stops. Liquidity is unchanged, but the strategy still fails. The latter probably means that your strategy was at least partly luck.

There is nothing wrong with good luck, and it doesn't mean that your thesis is wrong or that you haven't identified an information advantage. It doesn't necessarily mean that luck was all you had. It just means that you haven't actually identified the systemic causality in your system yet. Maybe you were lucky enough to run it during a period where the macro market conditions were a natural fit for it. Maybe those market conditions have changed and you need to rethink it at a more primary level to reconnect the optimization to the new behavior of investors. Maybe investor incentives have changed in some meaningful way. Specifics are hard to say without knowing the actual model.

But, that luck might have been a part of your past success doesn't mean the system can't be revived. It may exploit some other investor inefficiencies exceptionally well and you may have some true systemic advantages over others. But the last thing you want to do is spend all your time fretting and fussing with the existing settings in a way that will simply over fit the model to some greater or lesser degree, thinking that's the only possible solution, and consuming vast amounts of wasted time as a result. An error like that is almost certainly driven by motivated reasoning.

Cognition and Stress

There is one final cognitive trap that I think is worth mentioning, and it has directly to do with emotions and stress. A great many of us have learned to master our emotions, but that doesn't mean we don't have any. If we subordinate those feelings and control our reaction to them, that doesn't necessarily make them go away. Emotions can come bubbling up in unexpected ways, and they can often do so in spite of our superhuman efforts to control our reactions to them.

I have a dozen close friends that have been managing money in hedge funds all their lives and drink no less than two bottles of wine, every single day. They're completely functional and it would never, ever effect their job performance. They arrive in the office sober every day, and never begin drinking until the day is behind them. But they have to address their stress somehow, and addressing it chemically is what they've settled on. No one does cocaine in the top tier of hedge funds, there is drug testing in many firms. But functional alcoholism among portfolio managers is probably more common than it is among accountants or salesmen.

Trading is a spectacularly stressful job, especially if you're managing a large amount of money. It's more stressful than you can probably imagine. I'm convinced that unless you have a natural predilection for managing a high stress occupation, like a test pilot or someone working in ordinance disposal, even if you have all the other relevant pieces, you're not going to succeed at trading. As I keep saying, being smart alone won't get you there. I've had a lot of opportunity to observe this. Either you have a natural stoic nature, or you'll end up one of the richest men in the cemetery. I don't believe it's a skill that can be learned.

Many people talk about how humbling it is when you first go to University after being the smartest person in your class and you learn that there are smarter people than you out there in the big wide world. I have a good friend for whom that did not happen. Instead, when he got to University he discovered that yes, there are much smarter people out there than he had ever met in his little town, but they were by no means smarter than he was.

All through University he managed to stay ahead of absolutely everyone with relative ease. This guy is a genuine outlier when it comes to smarts. He graduated at the very top of his class in what can arguably be called one of the most demanding programs in one of the three most prestigious Universities in the world. He was a STEM grad of course. He went for hard sciences, Math and Physics all the way.

His professors, not a bunch given to false praise, described him as the single most promising mind they'd seen in a generation. And he was handsome, charming, and genuinely humble to boot. His professors were all deeply disappointed when he went on to Business school instead of a Master's program which would have led him to a role as their peer. His deeply practical parents on the other hand, were over the moon with his choice.

As you would expect, his Business School choice was the very top of the top, and he excelled there too with an ease that frustrated his peers. Luckily, he had enough natural charm to avoid fostering much resentment among them. He breezed through it, again at the very top of his class, and was immediately offered multiple competing roles in each of the biggest and most prestigious Investment Banks.

They all wanted him so badly that competitive promises were made to him, well in excess of the traditional starting role. He chose one he felt was best and set to work with all the other genius recruits as a Quant, where his stunning mathematical brilliance could be put to best use. To all eyes he seemed like a natural in trading, and to a great extent he was. He was a golden child, destined for greatness.

I didn't know him early in his career. I was on a similar (albeit much more modest) career path in a different bank. He and I wouldn't meet for several years. Eventually we both decided to leave the sell side and we met as Portfolio Managers at a hedge fund run by a legendary titan in the industry.

We were operating in different markets, me in equities, he in currencies, but we were both quants and became fast friends. Most days we'd find a few minutes to chat about this or that. Wives, kids, cars etc. You know the drill. Over time we became quite close.

When you're hired as a Portfolio Manager in an existing fund, you always start out with a small amount of capital, and as you demonstrate that your strategy is delivering the necessary return you are periodically reviewed, and given more. We started within a few weeks of each other, and he and I were both allotted 10 Million to start. In a few months, the head of the department came around, did a review of each of our strategies, and we were given a larger allocation – both on the same day - 50 Million dollars each.

The next day I did what most people would probably do, and traded 5 times the volume. Of course, this meant that not only was I making 5 times the amount of money on average, but periodically I would also take losses that were 5 times as large. In the case of my strategy that meant 'tail event' losses well over a million dollars on a single day. If you come from a comparatively modest background like I do, I can assure you that you don't really know what it feels like to lose a million dollars in a single day, until you do.

I'd like to say with traditional hedge fund bravado, that I was unaffected by it but it isn't true. Eventually I did get to the point where I could lose a million or even 10 million, and still sleep like a baby. But that first time I have to confess, it was a shocker. In the space of a single 390-minute open market session I lost more money than my father had made in 20 years. Enough money to buy brand new Lamborghini's for each member of an entire basketball team. Enough money to buy the entire block I lived in as a kid, twice. And that money was gone. Gone forever. It wasn't going to come back.

Right now, you're reading me talking about it and it seems like trivia to you. But imagine never having anything close to that much money. Imagine watching your P&L every second of the last hour of trading. Seeing the big negative number grow larger, and larger. First, it's the size of a few cars, then your house and car, then your neighbor's house. And then finally and painfully, freezing in place, with many more digits than you like. It's the biggest real world negative number you've ever seen in your life. That very first time, it's hard not to imagine that you're anything but the first person to lose that much, and that you're looking at the last moments of your entire career.

You've invested an amazing amount to get where you are. In my case it was well over a decade. There were those insane 100-hour work weeks at JPMorgan. Being awakened at 3AM at Moore because some database in another hemisphere had developed some glitch and someone needed to be told what to do. Getting endlessly chewed out by trading prima donnas who were blaming their mistakes on you, and taking garbage from emotional incontinents in operations who lashed out at everyone. Spending two years gathering data and then nights and weekends building a system, all while being criticized by a CFO who demanded that if I was going to work in the office on the weekends, I should be doing work that he wanted done instead of my own research. And finally, after nearly superhuman effort, convincing my bosses boss to vest the strategy - making vicious, nasty, extremely well-connected enemies in the process. And now, thanks to a few tiny blips on a screen, all that is going to be over, forever.

No one will hire a PM whose lost money, so there will be no upward place to go. Even worse, since you've been a PM there's probably no going back either. No one will hire you in a research role after being a PM because they'll assume you still want to trade. Even if you tell them different, no one will believe you. You've struggled mightily to get to this spot and now just a few weeks in, you've taken a massive loss, and it's all over. Finished. Forever.

The way your wife is spending money you'll be homeless inside a year or two. Not that she'll still be your wife for very long. With the family courts being what they are, god only knows what that will cost you. Maybe you can get a job as a golf pro someplace, or tutoring high school kids in math. Your cars are leased so there is no ability to sell and downgrade. With no cash flow, you're going to have to chew through the entire expense. Eventually she and your 3-year-old daughter will just have to figure out how to make it on their own. Maybe they can move in with her parents while you sleep in the street. The Route 18 bridge seems like it's pretty dry underneath. All this is the stuff that goes through your mind.

There was no such catastrophe of course. I wasn't fired. I wasn't even questioned about it. My bosses knew precisely what to expect from my strategy, and were totally un-phased by that first million-dollar loss. I never even got a phone call. And sure enough, the very next day I made back the entire million, plus a few hundred thousand besides. Some tiny technical details relating to slippage aside, the system was working exactly how it was supposed to work. My bosses knew it, in the end I knew it, and it all worked out just fine. I went on to trade that system for many years afterward. I even went on to change firms and negotiate myself a better deal.

Meanwhile my top of the top, golden child genius buddy who I'm unashamed to say was much smarter than I was, had a different experience. Like me, he knew his strategy was going to have a few technical concerns with larger scale trading as well, so he wanted to address them before he went live with the new capital. He had no interest in going through what I just did. He kept his positions at the small size while he knocked out the minor programming changes.

I checked back with him a few days later. He had found some other small issue and was still tinkering. A few days afterward, and there were more tiny details to address. Long after I was trading the larger asset pool and had learned to cope with larger gains and losses, he was still working with only 10 Million.

The other 40 million remained unutilized in the account.

Eventually our boss circled back around for another review. She and I talked about my strategy, and she was largely supportive. She had a few issues here and there, but after a little quibbling about certain performance properties and what to do about it, my allocation was increased to 100 Million. My buddy got a completely different conversation.

When our boss went to him, they were all hard questions. Why hadn't he increased his position sizes like he was supposed to? His capital had already been increased for the firm, so his returns had technically dropped dramatically. What issues were holding him back? Did those issues represent a material impact to performance? All the details were pored over. He told me later that he felt like he was really getting the third degree. She was smart, maybe the smartest human I'd ever met. She was a great person, but she was also very tough. She wasn't having any of his excuses.

In the end, our boss was unconvinced about his reasons for delay, so she laid it on the table for him. He was told that the fund had no room for all the costs associated with a small strategy and if he wasn't comfortable running the strategy at a larger size, then it would have to be shut down. They talked about the remaining development, and she gave him 5 more days to tie up the loose ends in his code and pull the trigger on the 50-million-dollar allocation.

What was happening in my friend's mind was a reaction to stress. He had always found his way in the past by hard work and superior intelligence, so to him, that's what it felt like he was relying on. He knew how to control his feelings, and he always did so superbly. But it doesn't mean he didn't have them. But to him the idea of much more substantial losses looked like peering over an abyss. He wanted to use his natural intellectual advantage to eliminate the problem before he ever had it, in the same way he had always done in the past. He was in essence, trying to trade more intellectual horsepower for the emotive pain that might come from greater losses.

His emotive mind had conspired against him to convince him that there was always some technical concern that looked important whether it actually was or not. He genuinely believed these were real concerns. They might have been. But the boss, who had seen these issues before certainly wasn't convinced.

As I'm sure you've inferred by now, he never made it, and his strategy was terminated, as was his position. An industry golden child, by far one of the smartest men I've ever met. Today he's in a front office support role where he has no P&L responsibility. He's paid very well, but only a fraction of what he stood to make as a PM, far less than he would have eventually made as his status in the industry was raised to the heights that everyone assumed would eventually be his.

It would be a mistake to say that this was a component of his character that held him back. It's more complicated than that. He wasn't lacking in courage. He's one of the finest men I know. One of the most disciplined scientific thinkers I've ever met. It's just that whatever the emotional component is that's required to make the big bet, it was the one thing missing from his personality.

He didn't drink too much or beat his wife. He didn't even fly off the handle at people, a common enough thing. But when the real stress of the position arrived, it turned out to be something other than what he imagined it would be, and his brain would have none of it. So, it spun him down a rabbit hole of believing that he wasn't quite ready yet.

This error is a recognition that at the bottom of our cognition is a creature which is by default, emotive rather than logical. Reason may be the application software, and that software may be fast, reliable and mostly bug free. But down below it, closer to the hardware, the operating system is emotion. There isn't any real way around it. It's true for all of us. And I'm convinced that the only way to override it to the degree required for this job is nature rather than nurture.

The astronauts in the Gemini program called it "The Right Stuff". English doesn't have a good word for it, maybe the Germans do. But whatever it is, you have to have it before you set out on this road. You have to be able to live with the fact that every single day that you walk into the office, it may very well be your last. Ever. There is success, and there is oblivion. There is no backup.

I know I've told you one story about what the stress is like. I say this with absolutely no fear of contradiction – I'm dramatically understating it. It truly is more stressful than you can imagine. Unless you've been in actual military combat and up to your ankles in hand grenade pins, I don't think you have any frame of reference for what it's like.

Owing mostly to my misspent childhood in a fairly dangerous environment, I've been in multiple life-threatening situations before. In the heat of a moment like that, it's comparatively easy to simply shut off the parts of your brain that might prevent you from doing what you need to, in order to ensure your survival. This is different. This is a grind. A slow slog. And you need a different kind of discipline to deal with the sustained and continual stresses of coping with a job like this.

Unfortunately, I don't know any way for you to really figure out if you have what's necessary to do this job or not, until you actually need it. I can't think of a way to truly test yourself for it. I can say that it's certainly no negative reflection on you if you don't. It's laughable to think you can get by on this personality characteristic alone in the hedge fund world, but it might be just as laughable to think you can get by without it as well. More than any other aspect, I believe this is simply something you're born with, or you aren't. And it might very well be that the real reason running a hedge fund pays so well, is because so few people are born with it.

The Next Big Thing

Although it's really a topic which is far too complex for an introductory book like this one, it would be impossible to finish up without saying a few words about Machine Learning and AI. But if you were reading carefully, you've probably realized that I've already spoken to many of the issues concerning these systems.

Most of what's called AI on Wall Street actually isn't AI at all. It's just a standard statistical predictive model with a machine learning component, which nine times in ten, is simply used as a tool to refit variables on the fly. You design the information model, you lay out the interactions of the various components, and then you rely on the Bayesian machine learning to determine if it's a 3-day RSI or 4. In very nearly all cases it's nothing too ground breaking. It's more a strategy marketing ploy than a groundbreaking change to the industry.

Like other models you might get lucky for a period of time. But having a bit of machine learning code iterate over a set of numbers which are nothing more than fitting (usually overfitting), probably isn't going to get you where you want to go. And this description applies to about 99% of all systems currently being run that say they're using AI.

Very few words I've written in this book will make people as angry as that last paragraph. I'm essentially calling a whole bunch of people out there, maybe not frauds, but something close. It's my opinion. I stand by it.

But I also know from direct experience that they aren't all frauds. And whether I'm right or wrong on that particular percentage is secondary. Because now that I've seen it first hand, I know for certain that true AI systems are much less well understood, and much more powerful domain than most people on Wall Street think, so we shouldn't let the present generation of systems be the thing that we judge the entire field of technology on.

No one has been guiltier of jumping to incorrect conclusions about AI's use in trading than I have. I've written a number of essays in the past that were very critical of the idea. With that said as a kind of mea culpa, the things I've observed in the last 18 months have convinced me that I was wrong about AI's future in trading, and when it finally comes to fruition, AI is very much going to be a part of the future of hedge funds. In fact, I think in the relatively near future, which is to say the next 15 years or so, someone, somewhere is probably going to write what turns out to be the very last computer trading program ever built, and when they do, they'll do it using a true AI.

The reasons I've changed my mind are several. First, where the industry used to require personal accountability for all risk decisions so there was always a specific individual to hold accountable, reduced average hedge fund performance thanks to increasingly efficient markets, has inspired many allocators to go a bit further outside the box. The industry wants higher return and if they have to consign a portion of their risk tracking to a black box in order to get it, many allocators are now prepared to do so. I never saw that coming. Maybe I didn't give them enough credit. These days, allocators are scouring the earth looking for a truly workable AI system. A great many of them are not only open to it, but have learned a bit about AI themselves and are actively seeking it out.

Based on my immediate experience, I think the level of interest is outpacing the level of familiarity, and most allocators still believe AI is a form of magic. You get a bunch of smart people together with a really powerful computer, add in a bunch of data and poof ... out come a parking lot full of Lambos. It doesn't work like that of course, but for them it's a numbers game, so that shotgun approach may get them there eventually. Most allocators have been taking a similar approach to the quant space for a long time. They never understood that particularly well either but it seems to have worked out OK for them.

That was certainly what I saw as the greatest obstacle to implementing AI in trading - how the industry viewed its own priorities and preferences. But that objection is largely gone now. Since it's no longer a concern, other more traditional obstacles similar to those that I've detailed here, are standing in everyone else's way.

If you hopped in your time machine and went back to 1966, to the first day the NYSE got a fully computerized trading system, you'd have to wait around for a good long time before you could put together a team of people with all the skills and knowledge necessary to build even the most rudimentary stat-arb system. Statistics wasn't new then, nor was market finance. But they were both domains of experts, and those sets of expertise didn't overlap at all. in 1966, you could find plenty of people who knew one or the other, but there were very few people alive who knew even the most rudimentary things about both.

Even if you could, before anyone could learn what they needed to in order to move forward implementing a stat arb system, they would have to unlearn a whole bunch of others things that the industry was then treating as sacrosanct.

The people in trading aren't really any different than the people in any other field. A little smarter and more mentally disciplined, maybe. They're certainly more objective on average, and less prone to emotional decision making. But one thing they have in common with everyone else, is that they all make assumptions. And in trading many of those assumptions revolve around believing that what is true today will remain true tomorrow, and for all time. In 1966, a great many ideas about how market finance worked, were spoken of in terms of final absolutes, and there were a ton of experts and vast business interests, all highly motivated to keep it that way.

These days, institutional traders at least, look back on what were viewed as the permanent and unchanging rules of finance in 1966, and chuckle. We've replaced what can be analogized as the financial alchemy of 1966 with a set of practices which are much more akin to particle physics. In that regard, the rules of today produce much more finite and accurate answers.

Yet one thing that hasn't changed much is that the industry still assumes that NOW we've finally arrived at the base level of truth about markets. We think we've found the maximum level of precision for description of risk. It's hard math, probability, and regression. It gets no lower on the logic chain than math. Math is pure, and absolute. We've got it! This is it! Finally!

Hard math and statistics are beautiful and elegant tools. But I've seen the best tools in the world used to build the most horrible structures. Just because you've got good tools, doesn't mean the thing you construct with them is any better than something woven from reeds and cut with sharp stones.

So, if you think this is as good as it gets with risk description, color me skeptical. When I look at the present state of quant finance, I imagine that the circumstance in 1966 was very similar to the one we have now, but with different knowledge as obstacles, different experts enforcing the current state of the rules, and different knowledge representing the coming breakthrough. And I'm convinced that in 15 years or so, the situation will have changed enough to make multidimensional deconstructive risk analysis look as quaint and silly as the rules in 1966 look to us now. The tech changes with time. The incentives, the infrastructure, and the inefficiencies all change with time. The intellectual arrogance of the people involved, never seems to.

In 1966 when technical analysis and assumptions about "greed and fear" were still considered the most reliable kinds of thinking, intuition and individual expertise were totally unchallenged. The first guy that tried to build a system based purely on statistics probably faced a dynamic similar to what you can see in the movie "Money Ball" when baseball management made a similar change, diminishing the role of scouts. I can imagine a floor broker trying to explain that "it's about people, and people's feelings can't be measured with statistics." This is nonsense of course, but I have no doubt many believed it in 1966.

What we've realized since is that it wasn't that the answer was wrong, it was the question which was wrong. Quantitative analytics takes on the question from a completely different perspective, and in the process, produces a much more precise answer.

Today in trading, the statistics are considered the absolute rules of the road. That is at the moment, how we define the new question. It makes perfect sense to me that today's experts should cast the same suspicious and unconsciously resentful eye toward what's new.

So, what specifically is standing in the way of AI? Well true

AI is something completely different from what Wall street currently thinks it is. In order to make room for it, they'll have to think about systems in a new way. Not a way that violates past rules or that demand that they give up the control over risk that they have under the current quant thinking, but one that certainly approaches those questions differently.

Maybe the argument will be for a constructive risk management model as opposed to a deconstructive one. My former colleague Rick Bookstaber's latest book "The End of Theory" takes a look at some options. I have my own ideas on a path forward which deviate somewhat from Rick's perspective, as I'm sure do many others.

When the code is cracked though, that change in perspective will become just another strategy. One more bit of creativity applied to a known problem of risk control. If it's someone with a minimum level of financial credibility, then they will get an institutional foothold. And when they then provide the right degree of evidence to support their new view, their credibility will rise, and other institutions will follow their early investors. So, the model I've laid out here can, and inevitably will be applied to the trading with AI. In the end, it will be the credibility of the people offering it, that will be the biggest obstacle to its acceptance.

I'll tell you something else. It will take nothing even remotely close to a singularity level of self-learning system to get there. The markets are a machine, with a known set of inputs, a known set of outputs, and a known, if somewhat unwieldy, set of dependent and independent variables. Even today the theory of everything can be worked out to a pretty precise level. It's just the time and money required to pool all the data and resources required, along with the expertise to build the system that's really standing in the way. But those are real obstacles, so let me give you a bit more color on how I see them.

Right now, the people with the necessary level of financial credibility on Wall Street don't understand what true AI is and how it works. That's a big problem, but anyone successful in trading learns pretty deep humility as a necessity of their success, and they know how to question their own biases and assumptions, so eventually one of them will be able to think far enough outside any box. My good friend Marcos Lopez De Prado is an established leader in this space, and he seems to be on the right track to me.

But an even bigger problem is that the people who truly understand AI don't know even the very first thing about the capital markets. Worse, they come from a world that's mostly academic in its thinking, and are deeply vested in inspirational truth as opposed to reasoned truth, so humility is very much not an essential for them, quite the contrary. The "Vision" is what's most important to them. To hell with reason. Reason to them is pure heresy, and anyone who offers any is often viewed as being heretical. In their view "too stupid to truly understand."

Academics have a remarkably poor track record at achieving

success in hedge funds. And while this new crop of extremely intelligent thinkers are out there using scientific reason to solve the technical half of the problem, on the markets side, the only thing they have to bring to the table is magical thinking. For them it's all vision and revelation, all the way down. They've never worked in an environment that required anything else of them.

Complicating that further is the fact that the people who do understand what a real AI system is, are truly some of the smartest and most creative thinkers alive. Like many of you, they've been conditioned to believe that intelligence is more important than knowledge, so when it comes to ego, they make Elon Musk look like Mother Theresa. That's what they've been trained to see as the inevitable path to success. They think the vision is the hard part and implementation is for grunts.

The people working in AI at Google truly believe they know what you want for dinner better than you do, and Facebook will call you an immoral monster because you prefer blondes to brunettes. How do you think people with that kind of hubris will respond to being told that they don't really understand how the financial markets work when they are absolutely certain that they do?

They're smart. That's beyond doubt. And they're convinced that smart is all it takes. There's little evidence to support that view, but they're talking vision not reason, so evidence to them isn't all that necessary when determining truth.

To my knowledge, no one alive is currently in possession of all the knowledge and expertise necessary to build a true AI trading system, who is also in possession of enough markets knowledge to make it work in institutional finance. Many people have some of the formula, no one has all of it. And given how difficult their personalities are to work with, I don't think the gap is going to be breached very soon.

Even when it is, a true AI system will need to employ Alt-Data from news & social media, it will need an intermediary layer where it predicts economic statistics like the unemployment rate, target interest rates, and the other statistics that drive the macro markets. It's going to need capital flow statistics and depth of book data. It's going to have to look at all the information that every other class of institutional investor finds compelling, and those expenses add up very quickly.

Maybe it can be done in pieces, but it will eventually need access to virtually all available market data across every dimension, and as much of the other available data that's possible to consume. The data and processing power it's going to take will be very substantial, not to mention the amount of time and money that will need to be applied to crafting the specifics of the solution.

This might just be a question of friction, but all of that stuff is very expensive to keep around when it isn't turning a profit. So even if you are the one person who understands both AI and financial markets, and you can make that claim credibly, you're still in the unenviable position of having to find a way to cobble together all the money, and the several years of intellectual horsepower necessary to build it all.

If I went to Jim Simons or Ken Griffin today and somehow persuasively made the case that I was the guy who could do it for him, I'd still need to ask them to pony up the millions of dollars (that I would spend not invest) and then ask them to give me a half a decade or two before they asked me for a return. On my best day, I'm a mediocre programmer. So, there will also be a whole bunch in salaries for the very big human brains I'd have to recruit and hire. None of whom will know enough about markets to be useful to the person paying for their time, in any other way.

In swap parlance, that makes the whole proposition an option on a future return, not a clear cash flow. One mistake by me or any of the other many people involved, and it could very well end up yielding them zero. If it does, they won't be getting their initial capital back. When a conservative estimate of the total expense is an excess of 10 million bucks, that's a big ask for anyone in the business, regardless of their proven experience and past success. It takes an awful lot of credibility to get over that kind of bar.

Also standing in the way are all those AI geniuses who are currently out there with basically no understanding of markets, but thanks to their inspirational vision, are absolutely certain they do. That's the exact story they're currently trying to sell. Then there are the other guys who know finance, but the only part of their model that's using an AI is the name. When all those people's efforts lead to failure, as they inevitably will, the industry consensus will become that "AI doesn't work", and the bar for someone who truly does know how to solve the problem will only get higher.

Still, I think the law of large numbers bears out the inevitability of success. The skills, knowledge and personal disposition to become a hedge fund Billionaire were exceptionally rare in any individual person 40 years ago. Today they may be different skills and knowledge, but I believe they're equally rare – just like the transition of necessary skills that occurred when Wall Street began its computerization. But get a large enough sample of people working on it, and sooner or later, you're going to find an outlier. It's simply math. He may not be around just yet, but he's certainly going to be.

When someone actually achieves it, I think you'll be able to tell. Market inefficiency is going to fall to some irretrievably low number and the price you pay for any asset will be vanishingly close to the actual fair value at the moment you execute. Any time price deviates by enough for whatever reason to justify action, the system will correct it by buying or selling, and applying market pressure on the other side.

When that happens, the rules of finance will finally become the universal rules of the road, and anyone who thinks otherwise will have to pay the AI for the privilege of believing so. Put another way, the rules of human nature and human behavior will, some mathematical derivation aside, become the absolute rules of finance. There will be no more reasonable exception.

That will take the "opportunity" away from all the punters and gambling addicts who like to treat the markets like a slot machine, and they probably won't like that much. They'll certainly complain, and the press will do their best to attribute some dark aspect to it. But in the end, that's probably a net upside too. Those guys were only ever going to lose a bunch of money anyway.

And it isn't like prices will never change after an AI system is properly funded. There will still be humans empowered to make all kinds of key economic decisions about the future. Many of them will be irresponsible, stupid, and unethical. You'll still have a world filled with unintended consequences, graft, and malice. There will be people like Elizabeth Holmes and Bernie Madoff out there in the business world, and dim wit shortsighted politicians in government. Central bank chairmen won't suddenly become more careful, prudent and thoughtful about the future.

People, even the best informed, best intentioned people, will always make mistakes. And in trading, those mistakes will always lead to someone else's profit, just like they always have. It's just the AI is going to be capturing most of it. But Finance is a human business after all. And human error is the indirect reason that there is a hedge fund industry in the first place. That will definitely not change.

Last Words

I can't tell you how many young analysts, aspiring PM's, and Traders I've spoken to over the years while they were just getting started. When you do that enough, patterns in their behavior and their thinking start to emerge. They all have different ideas, and different starting points for their trading models, but the errors they make with them all have a similar kind of topology.

This happens because of what they have in common. They're all super smart, and super determined. But whatever they're individual expertise, they all fall for the illusion that the easiest path is the one they should take. For some reason, it doesn't immediately occur to them that this path is the same one that everyone else in the industry has also followed years ago.

They seem to believe that if I run a trading model, and then someone else comes along and attempts to do exactly the same thing I do in exactly the same way, they'll get the same profit. They don't see that in the financial markets, my having done it the first time, prevents others from doing it. If I buy 1,000 shares at a certain price and a certain time, those shares are no longer available for others to buy. Another 1,000 shares do not magically appear at that price and time for the person who is trying to emulate me. They will at a minimum, have to buy a different thousand shares, and those shares will be made available to them at a different price, and time. To the degree that I'm correct and profitable, I literally prevent others from capturing that exact same profit.

I've expressed this idea a dozen times here already, but I wanted to say it again in the plainest language possible. As I said in the opening, the language of finance makes the concepts being discussed seem quite opaque, and easy to misunderstand. A great many young analysts, excited over their new discovery (that isn't really new, but seems new to them) are all too anxious to have the words mean whatever they want them to mean in order to leave room for their new vision of how markets work.

After years of watching it, I came to the conclusion that new analysts all chose the easiest path because at their level of experience, it's the only one they can see. They're smart, but they lack the knowledge of what does and doesn't work. Experience eventually teaches them that, but only after they get around to trying the things that don't work. What I've tried to do hear is share enough experience to give them a window into which is likely which.

In a sense, every successful trading model is caught between a rock and a hard place. In a short-term model, your position sizes are small because of limited trading volume, so you need a lot of trading and a pretty high hit rate to get a lot of P&L. In a longer-term model, there is plenty of volume available for you. But you need a very effective hedge to mitigate the volatility you import into your positions with the larger trade size, and maybe an outside the box trade execution strategy to acquire it effectively. There is simply no way to avoid that. There is no innovative vision that lets you ignore those rules.

The path to success is to chart a course between short term Scylla and long-term Charybdis. Or rather, to structure your interaction in the markets so that you do so in a way that takes advantage of all the other people out there who are making various mistakes when they try to do so. If you're going to have a vision, then it should be one which forms a reasoned speculation about who is doing what, when are they doing it, and how are they doing it wrong in those circumstances. That kind of vision will leave profitable room for you. You aren't going to get that with a 22-factor filtering model that uses technical indicators, and a back test that iterates to optimize for maximum return over volatility.

So, what is the right path? Is it trading really fast? Maybe. High frequency traders aren't omniscient and their models have serious weaknesses which are closely tied to their strengths. There are enough holes in their business model that I was able to propose one strategy for you right here. It may work, it may not. But it is by no means the only idea that attempts to do so.

Is the right path for you using Alt-Data? Maybe, if you know enough about the data to get to a valid signal without wasting 40 years wandering around the data desert chasing false ones. All of that information is going to have a ton of gems in it if you have the talent to mine them. Is the right path for you some new macroeconomic mechanism for market timing, or maybe some advanced hedging math? Maybe. I can't say for sure. And the reason I can't is that it depends on what you individually are good at.

None of us are the best at everything. A few of us believe we are, but we aren't. Trading will teach you that if you're capable of learning it. All the really successful people in the hedge fund world are absolutely certain of it. If they weren't, then they wouldn't know who to recruit to help them. No one gets to billions under management on their own.

There's a saying that an Investment Banking friend of mine repeats all the time. A's hire B's and B's hire C's and D's. It may work that way in the rest of the commercial world. But in the hedge fund world, A's hire other A's every chance they get. Even B's hire all the A's that are willing. They only settle for hiring B's when they absolutely have to. Only the most emotionally secure people are able to do that. But that's how you build a winning team in this industry.

Even now, after the mortgage crisis, after Covid, and after all the irrational top down decision making that has dominated post Obama America and the economic mayhem and catastrophe it's created, stellar success in hedge funds can still be achieved. It's being done right now.

I have a friend and former coworker who started a fund a

few years ago and is now at 11 Billion under management. He built that entire fund from scratch, and started it after 2008. Like me he's had a traditional career path for the industry which involved training at a big bank followed by time in a top tier hedge fund, so he has some advantages over you. But he got there during a period when few others could because he turned a reliable profit regardless of market conditions. On that score, you and he are on level ground. If he can do it, in theory at least, you can.

The opportunity is real for you, and it's out there. You just have to be aware of the same things he is. You just have to see the world the same way that he, and the rest of the institutional world does. Your aspiration is to make those people your customers, so you need to be providing a product that those customers actually want.

My friend understands his customer's concerns. He speaks directly to those concerns and doesn't try to impose his own vision. And he has an innovative way of delivering a solution to those concerns that leans very heavily on his own particular flavor of deep expertise. Now that he's been delivering for a while, he has massive credibility with his investors. Enough to justify as large an AUM number as pretty much anyone in the industry has ever gotten. In another half decade or so, you may be hearing his name and high school kids will be imagining being him.

It's not easy, but it can be done. If it can be done by him, and it has been, then maybe it can be done by you. The best and worst thing about the hedge fund industry is that as much as it ever really could be, it's entirely up to you.

For most people, I think this book will foster more questions than answers. There will be quite a few new concepts described here for the average reader and none of them are detailed in full. There are at least a thousand relevant details for each and every one of the concept I raised that will all matter to you eventually. My goal was to provide enough of the basics so that with a little careful thinking, the rest of the detail could be reasoned out. A decent analogy here is an iceberg. You get that it's made from ice, it has sharp edges, at least some of it is above the water, and most of it is below. But it's the part below the water that you will inevitably need to be worried about.

If you'd like to reach out with even more questions, there will be a blog to go along with the book at:
https://tcostell1.wixsite.com/my-site-1
I don't promise to answer everything. I'm not sure how much time I'll have for things like that. But if I get a question often enough or if the question is really interesting, then I'll do my best to throw something up on the blog for it.

Your best bet would be to think carefully first. Broad questions like "How can I tell if I'm overfitting?" are less likely to get answers. Highly specific questions which involved detailed knowledge about your strategy, will likewise probably get ignored.

And the best questions will be concepts that others might also benefit from hearing the answer to. Those that expose the topology if the big bluish-white object floating in front of your ship. With those, I'll do my best to provide a helpful perspective if I can.

About the Author

Tom Costello has been a 'Quant' on Wall Street for nearly as long as the word has been a job description. Working exclusively on the institutional side, his 30-year CV includes financial powerhouses JPMorgan, Deutschebank and Chase, as well as the legendary multi-billion-dollar Hedge Funds, Moore Capital, Tudor Investments and Caxton Associates. From his start on the JPMorgan Swaps floor in 1990, he's played an active role in the quantification of Wall Street. He's managed hundreds of millions of dollars both before, during, and after the 2008 mortgage crisis, and has never had an unprofitable year.

In spite of living in New York City, in his spare time, he occasionally shoots large animals with a bow and arrow. He swears that he always eats what he kills.

Made in the USA
Middletown, DE
18 October 2021

50523573R00195